AF256089

THE BEAUTIFUL BUSINESS

Alan S Adams

© 2015 Alan S Adams
LEGAL NOTICES

The information presented herein represents the view of the author as of the date of publication. Because of the rate with which conditions change, the author reserves the right to alter and update his opinion based on the new conditions. This book is for informational purposes only. While every attempt has been made to verify the information provided in this book, neither the author nor his affiliates/partners assume any responsibility for errors, inaccuracies or omissions. Any slights of people or organisations are unintentional. You should be aware of any laws which govern business transactions or other business practices in your country and state. Any reference to any person or business, whether living or dead, is purely coincidental unless otherwise stated.

Every effort has been made to accurately represent this product and its potential. Examples in these materials are not to be interpreted as a promise or guarantee of earnings. Earning potential is entirely dependent on the person using the product, ideas and techniques. The author does not purport this as a 'get rich scheme.'

Your level of success in attaining the results claimed in the materials depends on the time you devote to the program, ideas, and techniques mentioned, as well as your finances, knowledge and various skills. Since these factors differ according to individuals, the author cannot guarantee your success or income level. Nor is he responsible for any of your actions.

Any and all forward-looking statements here or on any of the sales material are intended to express the author's opinion of earnings potential. Many factors will be important in determining your actual results and no guarantees are made that you will achieve results similar to anybody else's. In fact no guarantees are made that you will achieve any results from our ideas and techniques in our material.

ALL RIGHTS RESERVED. No part of this course may be reproduced or transmitted in any form whatsoever, electronic, or mechanical, including photocopying, recording, or by any informational storage or retrieval without the expressed written consent of the author.

"Claim Your <u>FREE</u> Business Builder Tools For Use In Your Clinic and Increase Your Turnover by 50% to 100% Without Spending More Money On Advertising!"

(£297 Total Value)

Details revealed below...

Alan S Adams, author and leading business consultant, is offering an incredible opportunity for you to improve the way you run your clinic, without spending more money on advertising, for <u>FREE</u>! Alan has used these systems to help grow clinics, cosmetic and aesthetic businesses for years, and he is so confident that they work, he always offers a **"500% Return On Investment or Your Money Back Guarantee"**. So claim your free tools today and discover:

- How to **quickly increase your sales by 50% to 100%** without spending more money on advertising
- How to **guarantee that your business grows,** with small changes achieving huge returns
- The **"Five Simple Steps"** to get you a plan, get you really focused, and get you building the lifestyle you deserve
- **Secret insider tips and techniques** to get more new customers, and get your past customers to come back into your clinic and buy from you again and again

- How to get **Free Business Building** tools that have helped countless other clinics grow, and that Alan uses with his private clients

Claim Your FREE Tools Now by Visiting:

www.TheBeautifulBusinessBook.com

Here's What People Say About Alan S Adams

"This is a must-read for anyone looking to sky-rocket their business. Alan doesn't just talk big picture but delivers some kick-ass actions that you can implement into your clinic immediately, which add money straight on your bottom line"
Charlie Hutton | Digital Entrepreneur | Author | International Speaker | As Featured on BBC

"Alan's passionate about pushing people to achieve more than they ever felt was possible, and this book not only encourages you to reach beyond your potential but it gives you the strategy and tactics to do just that"
David Hyner | Goal Setting Guru | Author | International Speaker | As Featured on BBC

"Alan has really helped me move the business forward - I don't think we would be where we are now without him. I've developed ideas that I never would have had the confidence to do on my own! Working with Alan has most definitely been a great investment, and I have no intentions of stopping working with him."
Sally Wagstaff | Aesthetic Clinic Owner and RGN | As featured on BBC

"This book contains very clear advice on how my business can grow, become more profitable, with less running around. There is a real strategy to it which everyone should be aware of and Alan really helps you to achieve this focus"
Maxine Mosley | Aesthetic Clinic Owner and RGN

"Alan's book is excellent for when you need to take stock and review what direction you and your business are moving in. It really helps bring clarity and focus to what you are doing"
Sarah Beasley | Hypnotherapist and Stress Management

Acknowledgements

I'd like to thank all of the people who have contributed their time and who have inspired me to write this book, so huge thanks go to the owners and operators of all of the medical, cosmetic and aesthetic clinics that I've had the pleasure of supporting over the last few years. As well as to my family, who motivated me to start this journey in the first place. Thanks too to the whole team at Zen Communications for your expertise, and insights, as well as your eagle-eyes.

A special note of thanks goes to Nigel Botterill, Richard Reed, Peter Done and Johnathan Winchester for sparing the time to be interviewed for my next book on the mindset of the super-successful. Thanks also to Hilary Devey for agreeing to be interviewed next, and to Richard Branson, Nigel Botterill, Theo Paphitis, Deborah Meadon, James Dyson, Kelly Hoppen, Laura Tennison, and Rob Law who, although they couldn't squeeze an interview in, did take the time to consider the request and to respond so positively.

A final note of thanks to my beautiful partner Felicity. I wouldn't be where I am now if it wasn't for you, my beautiful newborn son Alexander, and thanks to my daughter Ellie who's taught me so much – no matter what, I'll always love you.

Foreword

With medical, cosmetic, and aesthetic clinic owners now facing more competition than ever before - and from overseas as well as on their own doorstep - it's certainly tougher than ever before to be in the business. And yet a few simple-to-apply techniques have the potential to help you sky-rocket your clinic's success, and to live the life you've always dreamed of.

Alan S Adams is a renowned business coach, author and professional speaker, and with his support and guidance hundreds of business owners just like you have moved their business from surviving to thriving. In this book Alan will show you how, with a few nips and tucks, you can make your clinic the ultimate beautiful business.

Raymond Aaron | New York Times Best-Selling Author

Contents

Sculpting Your Dream Clinic

If you're reading this then you'll know that we've moved on from the traditional 'build it and they will come' philosophy. In the good old days you could place some adverts in your local paper, Yellow Pages and then if you want to be really flash, you could do some radio advertising, then sit back and wait for the clients to turn up.

However none of us can rely on being the only provider of our service or product any more. In fact, we're not just competing with the clinic down the road, but those overseas too, and the market has never been more competitive. But believe it or not this is great news!

And it's great news because a lot of your competitors are still using traditional methods, in how they operate, market and position themselves, better still they're even doing them poorly. Only the other day I saw a billboard advertising for a beauty clinic, the billboard had the name of the clinic emblazoned across it and it was in a prime location. I'd imagine the owner would have been pleased as punch as they were getting their name out there and it was probably a big chunk of their marketing budget to get designed then hire the space. Unfortunately it's highly unlikely that this would have actually driven any footfall to the clinic, there was no call to action, no offer and there wasn't even a phone number. All the billboard advert was good for was some brand awareness and unless you're one of the corporations with a massive budget, it's a complete waste of money.

Also there are smarter ways of engaging with clients these days, through the use of social media, websites, pay per click adverts, downloads, strategic partners, the list goes on and on. However, again you'll see these mediums being used in a poor and ineffective way not just by the owners, but by so-called experts in the marketplace, so don't think hiring somebody can fix your problems marketing wise, you personally have to have a grasp of what works and doesn't work.

However the one good thing is that competition clears out all but the best business in the end, and if you follow the tactics we share in this book, then you'll absolutely be at the top of your game and you'll stand out for all of the right reasons.

The strategies and tactics we share absolutely work and every clinic I've ever worked with that has embraced these, has grown substantially. I've packed this book with ideas that I know will assist you in growing your clinic and pushing it to the next level, whether you're working on your own or have a team working with you.

You and I are where we are because of how we think. If you want to achieve more, do more, and be more, you have to think differently. I've invested £tens of thousands studying how successful business owners think, and I'm currently working with a millionaire who's grown a number of £million plus businesses, as well as a multi-millionaire who has over 40! Their ongoing mentoring and training programs have helped me to refine the skills and mindset to be super successful, and that's what I'm passing onto you here.

Ever heard the saying 'nothing worth doing is ever easy'? Bombshell alert – if building a clinic was easy, everyone would do it. It takes a certain amount of courage to become financially responsible for yourself, and it takes even more courage to be disciplined enough to do the things that others aren't willing to do now, to secure your financial future.

And if you're employing staff, you're financially responsible for them too. Their mortgages rely on your business and your decisions. If you haven't already been through tough times, you'll probably be in for some, whether its challenges with cash flow, waiting on decisions from others as to whether you get that dream client, or just plain and simply being let down by people.

You're likely to wake up in the middle of the night at some point worrying. You may feel stressed and lacking energy, and you might even be thinking "I'm not sure how much more of this I can take" or even "is it all worth it?" Well, you're not alone. Literally every successful business owner has been through this. Even Richard Branson has walked the streets of London at 3am because he was worried about what was going on within one of his businesses. Ultimately though, we all need to learn that if it's within your control, do something about, and if it isn't, stop worrying about it and focus on something that you can affect.

Unfortunately, running a clinic isn't all about the treatments;

you have so many different hats to wear that a lot of the time the treatments almost get in the way of building your business, while you deal with marketing, admin, unreasonable customers, cash flow keeping you awake at night (not sure who said this, but you know you have a business when you're awake at 3am wondering if you've still got a business). Being in business is a minefield for the caring soul and none of the training you did to get you where you are now ever prepared you for the turbulent seas you can find yourself in.

Now, I ride an old 1978 Triumph Bonneville and I've spent thousands of pounds and hundreds of hours on it, making it go quicker, improving the handling and – importantly with an old bike – making it brake better. I've even had it out on a few track days chasing much more modern bikes. Riding a bike is a skill and it's something that I'm okay at. I just love going out for a ride and getting in the zone where you're completely engaged in the present moment and you simply don't think about anything else. Buddhists would refer to it as mindfulness and living exactly in the present; I just think of the huge smile I always have on my face.

But it makes me really marvel at just how incredible professional bike racers are – they almost seem to defy the laws of gravity, and their focus is something every business owner and entrepreneur can learn from. I've been to the Isle of Man TT races a few times (if you've never heard of the TT races do look them up; it's road racing at the extreme). Motorbikes touch nearly 200mph and race around a 37.9 mile track made up of the island's own roads, which in all honesty are at best just B roads, complete with all of the street furniture, telegraph poles, walls and even houses you'd expect. If you've never seen any footage of these races you can see some bike camera shots on YouTube, and it just shows the speeds, which are phenomenal. Anyway, how these racers learn this incredibly long and complicated track, and how they take in such a huge amount of information at the speed they're going is truly amazing. Of course, at these speeds, and on these roads, when something goes wrong it tends to go very badly wrong for the rider.

Just so that you can understand how the races work, basically, if you live in the Isle of Man during these events you tend to leave the island as it's invaded by 40,000 bike fanatics who get to watch their race heroes while they stand on the roadside, a mere 10 feet away from them in places. It's a great atmosphere with everyone wanting these heroes to come in safely, and glued to their radios listening to the commentary…

I recall an interview with a renowned racer called Guy Martin who was entered into the senior race at the TT a couple of years ago. Guy, an experienced racer, had complained that the front tyre kept pattering in corners at high speed (pattering means the tyre was ever-so-slightly bouncing and leaving the tarmac for a fraction of a second) which caused the bike to run wide – not good on a narrow road with brick walls and telegraph poles, at these incredible speeds. Anyway, Guy set off on the race and was doing well until he hit his third lap where he came into Ballagarey Corner at 150mph and the front end of the bike started to wash out.

A split second later the commentator was reporting a huge fire ball at Ballagarey and everybody's heart sank. Everyone on the island knew that this was the fastest corner of the track, and that Guy, if not killed instantly, was almost certainly critically injured. Even his pit crew, believing him dead, started packing away his belongings in the garage. However, on the run into the corner, Guy had what every successful person has, complete focus... In the split second that the bike started to run wide, Guy was focusing on where he wanted to go and, knowing he was heading for a wall, actually started to leap from the bike in an effort to stay on line.

Guy suffered broken ribs, bruised lungs, twisted ankles and fractured vertebrae, which is the equivalent of a scratch considering the speed at which the crash took place! The key factor that kept Guy alive? His absolute, unwavering focus, and as an clinic owner that's what you have to have if you are going to build something that has the impact on your life that you want and deserve to have.

The variety of different roles or 'hats' that you need to wear within any clinic, especially when first starting out, can be overwhelming, and many clinic owners and entrepreneurs freeze before they even start. When I'm giving talks I often share the tale of the university lecturer who, in front of his students, produces a large glass jar that he fills with golf balls. He then asks his students "is the jar full?" The students all agree that the jar is full but the lecturer then pulls some marbles out from under the desk and pours them into the jar...

The marbles fill the gaps between the golf balls, and again, the lecturer asks "is the jar full?" Once more the students agree that yes the jar is definitely now full, but the lecturer pulls out a bag of sand and proceeds to pour that into the jar too. He again asks the students "is the jar full?" and the students – who by this point are less inclined to say it is, sit quietly. The lecturer then pulls out a beaker of water and tips the water in the jar and again asks if the jar is full…

He points out that life is very like the jar – the important things are the golf balls and the marbles, with the sand and the water representing the other activities that we get involved with. If you're not careful, you can fill your jar with sand and water and leave no room for the important stuff. Business is the same. Too often we get wrapped up in the actual doing – serving the customer, designing something, processing the sale – and not working on the important things which will actually grow the clinic into something that supports us moving forwards.

Ultimately if you're looking to build a successful clinic you have to work towards becoming less of a doer and more of a business owner, and this requires just as much effort on your part as when you originally studied your creative trade. It's not easy to let go and is doubly hard if you're really good at what you do, as you'll struggle to find people as good or better than you and you may find yourself wanting to take jobs back.

I've seen this happen in quite a few clinics, where the owners expand and then become tempted to shrink again because the quality of what's being done isn't to their high standards and the excuse of "it's just quicker to do it myself" rears its ugly head.

I mentioned the power of thought earlier, and how you think is impacted by who you decide to mix with and what information you decide to consume. Just reading this book, even if you don't agree with everything, will stretch your thinking and no matter how hard you try you could never go back to how you thought before.

And this is something advocated by David Hyner. If you've never heard of him, he's well worth looking up. He's interviewed some of the highest achievers and most effective people from the world of sport, music, arts, politics and enterprise. All of these people had one thing in common and that was that they set massive goals for themselves, not what most of us are taught when it comes to goal setting; SMART, which stands for Specific, Measurable, Achievable, Realistic and Timely.

What David says is to set yourself massive goals and then start planning for them. You're going to be setting goals anyway so why not set bigger ones than you currently have, no matter what type of clinic you have? You'll be super busy anyway so you might as well be super busy actually building a larger clinic than you're currently thinking of. And that's what this book is all about. It's about pushing you slightly further than you're comfortable going, giving you the strategies and tools to develop a larger clinic than you would have built in the first place; and this all comes down to mindset.

Like many business owners you may be striving for a

lifestyle business which doesn't control you, you control it. You may want more time off, a shorter working week, more holidays and the business to work whether or not you're there. And that's perfectly reasonable - after all the true definition of a business is a commercial profitable enterprise that you can walk away from and it keeps paying you.

Yet so few clinics actually hit this target of having a lifestyle business - Daniel Priestley has met over 3000+ business owners, 70% of whom were struggling. And if you look at national statistics that's supported, with roughly 70% of business owners never making it past a £quarter million turnover. Daniel identified that the £250,000 to £300,000 mark was the tipping point for most businesses when they move from struggling to having a lifestyle business.

Interestingly, in his presentation Daniel showed that while businesses from £0 to £300,000 were mostly struggling, businesses between £300,000 to £2million were in a sweet spot, which is where the lifestyle business exists. Bizarrely as you go to the £2million-£10million turnover bracket, business owners were struggling again because their businesses were once again different beasts and needed different systems and processes put in place. Daniel described it as you employing people and you go from 12 employees to 13; the 13th employee causes fragmentation within your workforce, people start to form cliques and communication starts to break down. Normally once over £10 million turnover the lessons have been learnt and the systems put in place so the business owners are back in that sweet spot again.

So, your ultimate aim is to get the business working without you. I'm not saying you suddenly stop doing anything and retire (unless that's what you want), but you want to be in a position where you have choices about whether you are going to work or not. You need to know that if anything disastrous hits you, the clinic will continue on without you. More than likely, like the super-successful business owners I've been interviewing, you'll continue working hard within your business and it will become a pleasure, not a chore.

When I interviewed Peter Done from Peninsula (if you don't know Peninsula they're an HR company with over 1000 staff in the UK) he actually said to me that he didn't have to come into work anymore, he chose to come because he really enjoyed it. You may not have heard of Peter, but he and his brother Fred started the Bet Fred chain of bookies.

Peter shared with me a hugely interesting story of how he and his brother got started. During the early 1970s they were each managing bookies for somebody else, but felt that they could do better themselves. The two brothers managed to scrape together £2000 but they still needed another £2500 to buy a shop. Luckily the businessman selling the shop believed that Peter and his brother could make a real go of it and decided to loan them the remaining £2500, to be paid back over two years. It was a great stroke of luck but was led, no doubt, by their own belief, and the businessman's faith was paid back when they repaid his loan within just six months.

They bought another shop, so each brother had their own to run, then bought a third and they got their sister to run that one. He said that unfortunately they started to hit problems at this point as they'd run out of family members to run the bookies they wanted to acquire.

So, they had to develop a system where the bookies could, with minimal input, run themselves. Peter and his brother continued to buy bookies, just repeating the business model each time, putting the systems in place to make each one run smoothly. Peter and Fred were still working seven days a week but their business was starting to compound massively with the effort they had put in developing systems, and by the early 80s they owned about 70 bookies. At this point, in one of the shops they took over, an employee didn't want to work for them and took them to court.

Fred and Peter took advice from a solicitor and even though they followed it to the letter, the solicitor ultimately told them due to a technicality they'd probably lose the case and should settle out of court, which they did for about £4500 (which in the 1980s was a considerable sum of money). Then, to Peter's surprise, even though they'd lost the case and a substantial amount of money, he received a bill for over £4000 from the solicitor.

A week later, Peter was approached by an HR company that offered to look after all of their HR needs and policies in the future to keep them compliant, plus reduce the chances of them being taken to court again, and if they did, as long as they followed the advice there was an insurance policy that would pay out for any court costs. Fred and Pete were so impressed by the setup of the HR company that they told the owner to give them a call if ever he needed investment. Six months later he did, and they invested.

Moving forward three and a half years, Peninsula was losing money hand over fist, and Peter and Fred's accountant told them to pull out and not to invest any more money. Peter spoke to his brother and said that he'd go into the company for six months and see if there was anything there they could salvage or do to push the business forward. When Peter examined what was going on he saw that there was a great team, but very little in the way of a systemised marketing and sales process. He rolled his sleeves up and went to work selling Peninsula products on the road for 7-8 months before he came in-house, set up a team, with a marketing and sales process, (including tracking their ratios so they knew what numbers they needed to do to hit their targets) and the rest is history.

What I see when I go into clinics is exactly what Peter saw when he went to Peninsula. Great people but a lack of systems, especially around the marketing and sales sides of the business. You'll hear people describing how their clinics are growing organically as if it's a good thing. In all honesty, I'm sometimes concerned by the use of this term, as a lot of the time it means that new clients are coming on board not because of a robust marketing system or strategy, but because somebody is referred by somebody, who referred somebody to them. Although new business and referrals are great news when they happen, it's very difficult to repeat, and anything that's difficult to repeat should cause you some concern. Clinics can also rely too much on one type of marketing, which is dangerous as, should something happen to that one marketing pillar, you'd be vulnerable. The classic is the clinic that ranks number one organically on Google, only for Google to once again change their algorithm and they drop off the face of the world.

Using a number of marketing pillars that all work together to feed clients in to you, and which you should be able to track and measure the return on investment for each, is what your clinic should be aiming for. That way you can predict your future clients, and can grow and scale.

Getting More Done

A recent article I read said that office workers, because of the array of social media available, including Twitter, Facebook, Pinterest, Google Plus, and YouTube – to name just a few – plus texts, phone calls, and people popping in or asking questions, are interrupted once every 11 minutes! This is shocking enough, but when you consider that getting focused on what you're doing can take around 25 minutes before you're 'in the zone', many office workers can spend their entire day without ever really being able to focus on anything that they're doing.

Can you imagine how that can impact on any clinic's output? While the treatments themselves are uninterrupted, when engaged with all the other important tasks to grow your clinic your productivity is being destroyed. Plus, I'm pleased to say that the idea of being able to multi-task and switch between jobs has been debunked, with recent studies showing that your IQ drops by ten points each time you try, compared to smoking marijuana which only sees it drop by five points. That's right, you're better off smoking a joint at work than trying to multi-task.

If you still don't believe me, try this next exercise. I want you to write out, "multi-tasking is a lie", and then number each of the letters. In the first exercise I want you to write the letter M then the number 1 underneath, then the U with the number 2 below, and so on. I want you to write it as fast as you possibly can, timing yourself as you do it. It should look like the example below.

M U L TI T A S K I N G I S A L I E
1 2 3 4 5 67 89 10 11 12 13 14 15 16 17 18

Then I'd like you to do the same thing again, but this time, simply write out the statement "multi-tasking is a lie" first, and then write 1 to 18 under each of the letters afterwards. Seriously give it a try now.

The second time you were probably a third quicker than the first, which demonstrates how impractical multi-tasking is.

So, why have we focused on all this up front? I deliberately chose to include it early because if we can simply squeeze an additional 30 minutes out of your day, that would give you around an extra 15 working days a year. And that's about a month that you don't currently have! I really believe that if you nail this, you'll be far more efficient and have a lot more time to play with than that.

Remember that if you're saying yes to something you're saying no to a lot more other things. Yet it's an easy thing to do. Someone asks if they can sit down with you for five minutes and pick your brains (when is it ever five minutes?) and you think 'yeah no problem' I'm a nice person so you say yes, but what are you ultimately saying no to? A lot of the time it's the really important actions that get pushed back.

You need to focus on the important things, and don't multi-task; in fact in Gary Keller and Jay Papasan's book <u>The One Thing</u>, they talk about the importance of niching down and concentrating on one thing that is ultimately most important to you in achieving success, rather than trying to achieve everything. You may have heard the saying "If you're chasing two rabbits, you won't catch either one."

'One thing' is in reference to an idea. Everyone should pick their own one thing and focus completely on it with no exceptions. Michael Phelps is used as an example in the book as he chose to practice for six hours every day, including Sundays, because he saw that that would give him a 52 day advantage a year over his competitors who were only swimming six days a week. And he became the most successful swimmer and most decorated Olympian of all time with 22 medals.

Steve Jobs was famously ousted from Apple by the then board of directors, before going on to completely revolutionise how Pixar worked, turning it into a company worth £billions. When Apple was in trouble the board of directors knew Steve was the man to turn them around, but insisted that he sell Pixar because they also recognised that he needed to concentrate solely on the one company. And what was one of the first things he did when he re-joined Apple? Dramatically reduce the number of Apple's products.

So, the one thing means extreme focus and a lot of work – one important thing at a time. The authors suggest that you should use the focusing question: "What is the one thing I can do, such that by doing it, everything else will be easier or unnecessary?" Answering this question and following through will cause a domino effect which will bring you success.

After you have picked your one thing, your first priority should be protecting the time you use to work with it. The authors suggest you should reserve four hours of non-interrupted time from your day only to work with your one thing. I'd say that four hours is a big ask for most clinic owners, but I would advocate at least 90 minutes a day, preferably first thing before you do anything else.

And that is the key to productivity. Uninterrupted focus. It's about blocking your time, staying focused on the task at hand, and making sure that all potential distractions have been managed so that they're less likely to interrupt you or distract you. It's also about understanding what's really important to your clinic at that point of its growth.

Nigel Botterill is a true entrepreneur in every sense of the word, and has built eight separate £million businesses. He uses this technique and he's so protective of his first 90 minutes in the morning that he has a "Do Not Disturb Unless There's A Fire" sign on his door. His team know that interrupting Nigel during this time is potentially a disciplinary issue, because those 90 minutes of being able to work <u>on</u> his business each day are so precious, and he knows they're absolutely critical to his future success. He's such an advocate of the 90 minute principle that he's just written a book called <u>Build Your Business in 90 Minutes a Day</u>, and talks about how you step closer to your ultimate goals in that daily time.

I met another super-successful guy a few years ago – Darren Hardy. His book, <u>The Compound Effect</u>, focuses on the little things you do every day, and how these small actions and choices can compound to have a huge impact on your life and business in five years' time. That may be negative, such as a few biscuits a day leading to a big weight gain over time, or positive in terms of reading a few pages of a book leading to significant learning and development. I think that Nigel's 90 minute habit is a brilliant demonstration of the power of this principle. Small actions, done consistently, every day, absolutely compound into hugely impactful outcomes.

This topic is typically referred to as 'time management', which when you think about it is a bit of a strange title. Everyone knows what you mean by time management, and you may have even paid to go on a time management course – I've run them myself – but let me share a secret… There's actually no such thing as managing time. (I usually save that nugget for my delegates after they've shown up… And paid!)

After all, you can't store time. Everyone has all the time there is. Nobody has more time than you in a day. Increased demand does not mean increased supply. And it's not flexible (ignoring Einstein's Theory of Relativity, for a while at least). What it's actually all about is self-management, and you'll have particular challenges depending on your circumstances and what you allow to distract you.

It might be that you procrastinate or avoid doing certain jobs – we all have distractions that can all-too-easily interfere with our day – but we simply need to make sure that we're in control. When you look, you might even notice certain emotional triggers that lead you astray, and running a clinic can sometimes feel completely overwhelming.

The trick is to break these tasks down into manageable chunks. In the book The Happiness Advantage by Shaun Achor he talks about Zorro circles. The story goes that when Zorro first set out to change the world, he wanted to do too much, too soon, and was overwhelmed by the tasks that faced him, sinking into depression and drinking. Then, our hero met Don Diego who decided to train Zorro. Don Diego drew a small circle in the sand and told Zorro to step into it. Only when he'd mastered that small circle would he draw a bigger circle that he could then learn to master, and slowly the circles got bigger and bigger.

Shaun talked about how we are all 'emotionally highjacked' when we feel stressed or overwhelmed, and that we need to focus on the small things we can do, because as we take these baby steps, we instantly feel more in control, and – as a consequence – happier.

It's a bit like asking 'how do you eat an elephant' or deal with any large project? The answer? One bite at a time! Simply cut it up into smaller pieces, prioritise the actions to be taken, and then create an action list and you'll slowly move forward until the elephant is gone and you've achieved your goal.

Are You Addicted to Urgency?

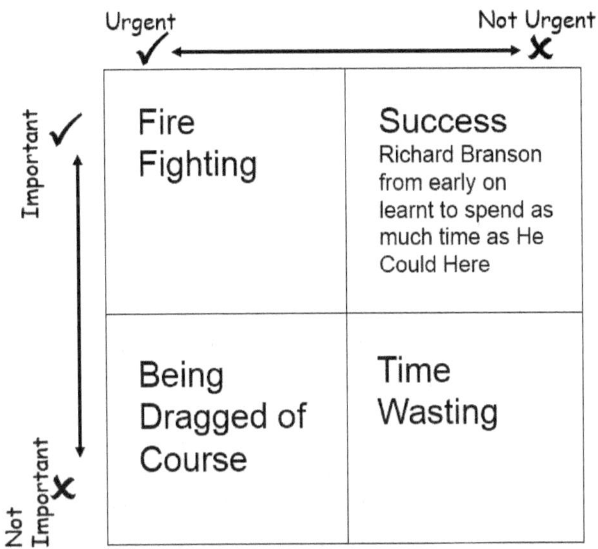

The chart above comes from Stephen Covey's book <u>The Seven Habits of Successful People,</u> but Covey actually learnt the principles of this from Dwight D. Eisenhower's <u>Decision Matrix,</u> something that Eisenhower used through his life as a General then President. He's even quoted as saying. "What is important is seldom urgent, and what is urgent is seldom important."

So looking at this chart, how much of what you do is in the ideal box of *not urgent but important*? That's success. The planning and information work which is essential for building your clinic. It's okay to cross over to the *urgent and important* box sometimes: clients may need prompt help, situations you can't plan for may occur, or on occasion you may need to change your plans at the last minute. But many clinical staff and owners actually spend too much of their day dealing with *urgent but not important* tasks like emails and some calls, or even worse, you may get some team members slipping into the time wasting activities like chatting by the water cooler or random social media activities that have no strategy behind them so are not driving the business forward.

Ultimately, one thing you do have to get good at is planning – that's the *important but not urgent* stuff – and this is where all the super-successful spend the majority of their time. You need a daily, weekly, monthly, and yearly action list and it will soon become a habit. It's something that you need to get your team involved with too, so that they understand what's important and why you're doing it. I always advise that you host a weekly meeting and then a once a month overview of how the strategies that you're employing are working and where you are as a clinic.

Depending on the size and type of clinic you're running, simply tracking what your team are spending their time doing can be critical. You may be using one of the industry-specific project management tools or even a paper based one, but if you've not really started tracking exactly where your clinics time is being spent yet, start now. There's a very simple project management and time tracking tool called Toggl that will allow you to track what your team are doing and for whom they're doing it, so it's worth an explore.

If you're looking to increase efficiency, though, where should you begin? It all starts with a routine, and getting you and your team to block out your day so that you focus on whatever it is that you need to be doing with no distractions. Schedule to pick up and respond to your emails just twice a day – perhaps from 10am till 11am, and 3pm till 4pm, then set aside some more time to return calls – you may wish to do this once a day but limit it to a maximum of three a day regardless. Then block out the rest of the stuff you need to do around this.

Take some time out to write out your perfect week and get your team to do theirs as well. A guide and template for this is included the pack of free bonuses I've put together for you at **www.TheBeautifulBusinessBook.com**.

You may be thinking 'I can't do that, my clients expect to be able to get hold of me' but just consider for a moment that unless you're a member of the emergency services or urgent response, it's highly unlikely that it's a genuine life or death situation. Plus, if your customers expect instant feedback, stop for a moment and ask yourself who's trained them to think that way…

Has anyone ever emailed you to say 'the building's on fire'? And how many issues need you to instantly respond on the phone? As long as you revert back to the client on the same day, or even within a few hours, it shouldn't be a problem. If it is, then set up an emergency email or have a dedicated line or mobile to deal with pressing issues (and if you can charge a premium rate for providing this, then make sure you do as it will make people think twice about using it).

And, with every email you receive, make sure that you deal with it as you read it the first time. Ask yourself the following questions and take these actions:

1. Does it concern you? If not, pass it on
2. Do you need to keep it? If not, bin it
3. Is it useful? Yes, file or read it, no, bin it
4. Does it need action? Yes, do it, and no, file it or pass it on.

Create a routine, set up files and systems for easy retrieval, and learn to scan and speed read emails and messages.

I don't often advocate using an answering machine to field and screen calls, as you risk potential customers hanging up without leaving a message, so why not consider using a professional telephone answering service? These are normally relatively low-cost, the staff are trained to answer the phone as you wish and take core information, then they email you details of the enquiry so that you can pick it up when it suits you better. And again, if it does require an immediate response, the call-handler can email an 'emergency' address where you can see and respond to it, or get them to call a specific number that you will be able to pick up. Imagine as an clinic, if you had your calls on divert every morning and spent that morning focusing on getting stuff done without any interruptions, how that would impact on your productivity…

Another great way to seize control of your day is to decide on, and put into action, bookends for your day. You can't often control every element of the main portion of your day, but you can control what happens immediately after you wake up and before you go to bed. You may decide to read a few pages of a positive book, to meditate or focus on your goals, or to spend a short period of time exercising. Perhaps you decide to listen to an audio book on your commute to work too. Activity first thing in your day is all about getting your brain into the right frame of mind and turning unproductive time into something positive.

Then, when you get into work, block off the first 90 minutes of your day to work on your clinic or an important project. Then and only then open your emails, answer the phone, return calls, or brief your team. If you have an office, put a Do Not Disturb sign on the door when you're working on one of your blocks of time. If you're in an open plan office, use some headphones and make sure that everyone knows not to disturb you. Hey, hang a sign on your desk so people know that you're working on stuff and don't want to be disturbed. You'll quite often find that one particular time of the day is when you're most productive, so use that time to do whatever activity you get the highest return on investment from.

At the end of your day you may decide to look back at what you've accomplished, perhaps note a few things down in a gratitude or acknowledgment list, and one thing I highly recommend is to write your To Do list for the next day so that you can hit the ground running. The choice is absolutely yours, but these bookends need to become a core part of your day and your teams' that are non-negotiable, and completed regardless of whatever else is going on.

If the first thing you do in the morning is open your emails, you're instantly allowing your day to be hijacked by other people – you're immediately marching to the beat of someone else's drum – and you may never seize back control. Do your bookends and you can rest assured that you're regularly doing something that is moving you forward towards your goals, no matter what else happens during the day.

Now, it's no good starting and ending your day well, and blocking out parts of your day for core activities, if you then have distractions popping up constantly. So, switch off your email alert, you know, that little box that pops up telling you an email has just arrived. No email should ever be so urgent that it has to be dealt with immediately.

Then, switch your phone on to silent and remove the vibrate function (and this includes alerts for emails, messages, calls, and all of your social media channels). You can check for messages every 90 minutes if you have to, and can schedule a call-back or response at the time you've allocated. To help you manage these interruptions, remember that they're taking you away from what you *need* to do, and so taking time away from what you *want* to do. Follow my five points below and start to free yourself:

1. Outsource incoming telephone calls and message-taking
2. Avoid small talk
3. Be assertive – remember it's okay to say no
4. Prioritise the interruption – how important is it really?
5. Develop effective telephone skills.

Also, look to delegate or outsource as many tasks as possible from your to-do list and schedule of tasks. It's likely that your time and your team's, admittedly depending on their role, is worth a minimum of £50 per hour, so why would you do a job that you could get someone else to do for less?

If – like many people – you struggle to let go of certain jobs because you believe that no one else can do it as well as you, ask yourself 'if my business was turning over £10,000,000, would I be doing this job?' Or, if you struggle with that one, ask 'if Richard Branson was running my business, would he be doing this?' If the answer is 'no', find a way to delegate it to someone else, outsource it, or create a system to take care of it.

Think about the skills that you need to run your clinic efficiently and think about your function and role. What action or activity gets left and becomes urgent and important? What are routine tasks, and what falls under the banner of administration? Then coach and train your team so that you can let go, and outsource whatever else you can.

Meetings have often been considered 'the practical alternative to work', and managing your meetings effectively is crucial in allowing you to take back control of your day. Meetings can be just the biggest waste of time when attendees get stuck on the smallest detail and can't or won't move forward. One tip I picked up is to focus on the minutes from the last meeting at the end, as you often find that many of the points have already been covered and you can whizz through them. Consider these tips when planning and taking part in meetings in the future:

1. Think about the meeting format. Does it need to be face-to-face or can it be done via some other medium like Skype or Zoom?
2. They should all have a set purpose and objective, and all attendees should be clear on what this is so make sure to share it
3. Set an appropriate time to start and to finish the meeting and agree it. Then stick to it
4. Set, prioritise, and circulate an agenda before the meeting
5. Make sure that you cover important items first, that way if you run out of time the core topics have been covered even if you don't discuss everything.

With your time management and allocation do also remember that it's not all about work, you have to look after yourself and your team's emotional well-being too. All too often people can feel overwhelmed by the sheer volume of what there is to do, and that's not just within the workplace, these principles work for home life too. A lot of people struggle with work-life balance, feeling guilty when they're at work because they're not with their family, then feeling guilty when they're with the family because there's some pressing work matters that they feel they really need to get sorted. Wherever they are they're never really present, so no wonder they feel stressed!

Being in control, or should I say feeling that you're in control, is critical to your clinic's productivity, your happiness and – as it turns out – your health. A 1997 landmark study conducted of 7,400 employees showed that those who believed they had no control over deadlines that had been set were 50% more likely to suffer with coronary disease, and that's as high a health concern as having high blood pressure!

In another study, a selected group of older people living full-time in a residential care home were given the task of looking after their own plants. This small responsibility and sense of control within their lives not only made them feel happier but it actually reduced mortality rates when compared with others in the same home who didn't look after their own plants and simply watched staff take on the task. Such is the importance of feeling in control that it can even prolong life.

So, it's important for you and your creative team to set and feel in control of deadlines. Remember we mentioned the Zorro circles earlier, well, make sure that you're not only supporting your team in how you allocate deadlines, but also how you actually set out these tasks to be done.

Ultimately, if we can manage our distractions and take back control over how we spend our time, we can become far more efficient at what we're doing. But – and here's the fly in the ointment – if what we're doing isn't following the right strategy in the first place, we still won't be getting anywhere, and we'll just be a lot more efficient at not getting there. Don't worry though, we'll cover strategy soon and make sure that you're on the right path.

Here are a few other things to consider for your wellbeing and that of your team:

1. If you're stuck on a piece of work, struggling for a killer idea, or can't quite word something for that important marketing, take some time away to do something else
2. Keep fit and focus on your health – you need a strong body and lots of energy to be at your best
3. Leave work in the clinic and make a mental divide between work time and home time
4. Take breaks away from where you work
5. Manage your negative self-talk, change 'should' to 'could' which acknowledges that you have a choice, and recognise that no one is perfect – just think how you'd react if someone else spoke to you as you speak to yourself
6. Focus on positive affirmations
7. Make time to see and stay in touch with friends and family – they're important.

Now this is where you go back to the 'Your Perfect Week Planner' you did earlier and plan in where all of these activities are going to take place. As far as possible these should be set in stone, as it's these activities that will ultimately get your clinic to where you want to be. I know it seems like extra work, but I promise you that doing this will put you in the top few % of clinic owners in the country. But don't be fooled. A lot of these activities may not yield results for months or even years, but consistently doing them will eventually allow you to catch momentum and then you are really going to start to shift.

One more thing; if you sometimes struggle to work out what the really, really important actions are then look at the jobs this way. If you have a task, say, to set up a system that will save you 30 minutes a month and it's going to take you a couple of hours to do it, that's an ultra-important task. Simply put, after four months the time will have covered itself and from thereon it will pay you back every single month. Your ultimate goal is to concentrate on getting your time back and working out a way to make your position redundant.

I was at a business event where I spent some time with New York Times' Bestselling author Raymond Aaron (who's kindly written the foreword for this book) and he pointed out something really profound. He said 'most business owners only have a single business so they can afford to be really inefficient with what they do. I have 40 businesses so I have to be really efficient with how I am with my time'. He went on to say that he has a one-week holiday every month and a one-month holiday every year. So, if you want to focus on anything, start working out the best way to get rid of the jobs you're doing.

Mindset of Successful Clinic Owners

Quite often I'll have people ask me "How do I get more customers?" "How do I develop better products?" Or "How do I make a £million?" I always ask "Why do you want that?" Often the first answer is "I want more money", but that's not likely to be the important bit, so I'll ask again "Why do you want that?" and they start digging around for a compelling reason as to why they're doing what they're doing.

There are actually two 'whys' you need to know to make building your super-successful clinic easier. The first is 'why are you doing this?' Consider what's in it for you. What is your end goal on a personal level? So, basically consider what lifestyle you want, where you want to live, where you want to travel, who you want to help, how many holidays you want to take, how many days a week you want to work...

And this is important on a couple of levels. Firstly, if you don't know what your end goal is, you can end up anywhere, and anywhere might not be a place you like very much. And secondly, your brain is incredibly powerful so you need it to be on your side. Quite often people will sabotage themselves without even realising they're doing it, and here's how it works…

Your brain, at its very basic level, has two parts; your conscious mind and your unconscious mind. Now your conscious mind can concentrate on seven things – plus or minus two – at any one time, while your unconscious mind, well, scientists still haven't worked out the exact figure but if you take the average of the different studies, you're looking at about 7,000,000 (and to have this super-computer to back you up and help you achieve your ambitions is pretty impressive!) However, there is a down side to this and that is that the unconscious mind is as dumb as a dodo.

It works with just a few basic rules and one of them is that it doesn't understand negatives, so, when it's presented with something it has to understand, it must first create it in order to be able to process it. Take someone trying to lose weight for an example. They may be saying to themselves "I have to stop eating chocolate cake" but all their unconscious mind hears is "eating chocolate cake" so it immediately goes to work and quite literally feeds the conscious mind with rich images of chocolate cake.

In fact it's likely to have even worked away in the background to deduce where the nearest chocolate cake is located and what the best way of getting it is (remember it can do 7,000,000 things at once – a rare case of multi-tasking actually working). In this scenario it's far better to concentrate on what you want to gain – say being healthy and slim – than what you want to lose, because then the unconscious will feed you more helpful images and help you work out how to achieve your positive goal.

Another example is – and for any parents out there, I can absolutely guarantee you've done this or heard other parents doing it at least once – a child is climbing along a wall and the parent shouts "Watch you don't fall." What does the child's unconscious mind hear? "Fall!" And it works out the best way to achieve this, runs rich images of it happening, and more often than not, helpfully follows through. Basically, it's imperative that you concentrate on what you want, and not on what you want to avoid.

Another statistic that I found really interesting in my research for this book is that 77% of self-talk is negative (you know, the little voice in your head that you have conversations with – and if you're sitting there thinking "I don't have a little voice in my head", that's it right there). If you're anything like me, you would never talk to someone else how you sometimes talk to yourself, so it's important to recognise what you're actually saying and how true that really is. To demonstrate this I'd like you to do a little exercise…

I'll describe a scenario to you and I want you to close your eyes and actually go through what I've described in rich detail. Ready?... Imagine that you're standing in your kitchen, it's a lovely warm day and sunlight is streaming through the window. You see that on one of the kitchen surfaces is a lemon, a chopping board, and a knife. You walk over and pick up the lemon, feeling it in your hand. It's cool, smooth and you can feel the slight pimples in the skin.

You sniff it and there's a light citrus smell. You place it onto the chopping board pick up the knife and cut the lemon in half, and as you do so, some of the lemon juice runs out and you smell the clean, sharp tang. You take one of the halves of the lemon and cut that in two, then you pick up one of the quarters, hold it up to your nose, and smell the sharp, bitter and fresh tang. Now, bite deeply into the lemon… Run through the exercise and no cheating.

What happened? Your mouth watered didn't it. And that's mad when you really think about it. Without wanting to go all 'The Matrix' on you, there is no lemon, and yet you had a physical reaction to something that quite simply didn't exist. It evidences perfectly how your brain doesn't know the difference between what you simply think and what you actually experience, so if you imagine negative things or say negative things to and about yourself, your brain takes them as absolute fact even though it might actually be rubbish (and is most of the time).

Why not make a note of any negative thoughts you're focusing on? Gather together a rough list and take just a moment to review it. A lot of the time, once you can actually see your thoughts for what they are, you can see just how ridiculous and harsh they can be. Why not try and replace them with positive affirmations, which are statements that make you feel good, or instead state goals you'd like to achieve?

For example, when I was writing my last book, <u>Survive to Thrive,</u> I wrote out a post-it note and stuck it front and centre on my desk, saying 'I am an Amazon bestselling author'. Now, I'm actually slightly dyslexic and sometimes my spelling is so bad that even my computer's spellchecker, whose sole job is to suggest correct replacement spellings, just flashes blankly at me with not a clue what I mean, so my brain could actually focus on a whole host of reasons why this could never be.

It could have called me out and told me that I'm a liar because, right at that second, it wasn't actually true. But, having really looked at some of the negative stuff I've said to myself in the past, I've decided that they were lies too, so if I'm going to lie to myself, it might as well be a good one! As it was the book did indeed become a bestseller here in the UK and the USA, so there's the power of positive thought.

The reason it's so important to start with these sorts of affirmations and watch the way that we think is because our brains have to delete, distort and generalise the world in which we live in order to cope with so much information pouring in from the outside world. To see what I mean, right this second, take a moment to concentrate on your left foot. Is there any pressure on it? Can you feel material touching it? How warm or cool is it? Now, all of those sensations and feelings have always been there but you didn't notice them before because your brain decided they weren't important and filtered them out.

These filters are shaped by the way that we see the world, and – as is our way – we get stuck into certain habits and so only see certain things. It's undeniably true that what you concentrate on, you'll find more of. If you think that everyone's out to get you, for example, your brain will find evidence of that to back up your thoughts. Or if you're looking for evidence that you're super-lucky, you'll find that too.

Depending on what you're filtering, you'll have a completely different experience of what's going on right now than the person sitting next to you. If you believe that it's really difficult to get new business, guess what, your brain will find loads of evidence to support that for you. How often have you been to the same party as someone else and you had an awesome time and thought it was the best ever, while they complained about the volume of the music, the poor food, or the rubbish company?

Whenever I sit down with a business owner for coaching, I always start with the end in mind. Their 'why'. Not long ago I was chatting with one new client about where they wanted to be in five years, and they were struggling a bit to answer as they'd never really thought about it before. To help, I started to ask specific questions to prompt their thinking process, and one of them was 'how much holiday time would you like to be taking?' They considered this then replied 'I'd love to be able to take a week's holiday.' I won't print my exact response, but a sanitised version is along the lines of 'are you crazy?' Can you imagine what would have happened had they continued with that line of thinking? Programming this super-computer with the thought that they would like a week's holiday in five years' time. More than likely, that's what they would've got and they'd then have been wondering, why, when they've worked so hard they can only get a week long holiday after five years.

During the recession in the 1990s there was an insurance company on the east coast of America and, like most businesses, they'd been hit hard and were struggling. One day, the owner came into work, looked around the office and noticed, not surprisingly, that the sales people were flat, the atmosphere was glum, and that it just wasn't a great place to be.

But then he had an epiphany. Even if these were good times, even if there was no recession, they would have practically zero business coming in because of everyone's attitude. And he went on to think that if his guys were like this, then the competition must be similar, which meant that no-one was out there actually selling to potential clients.

What he did then was to get the sales people in to sit down with him one at a time and he asked them to set some personal goals that they'd like to achieve financially – whether that was getting a new car, going on a great holiday, or making home improvements – he got them to concentrate on these positives. He went on to explain that the competition wasn't out there selling, so there was a huge opportunity for them to grab loads of businesses, and with the exception of one guy (who soon left) everyone was on board. And guess what? The company doubled its turnover, during a recession, and attributed the whole growth to simply thinking differently about their circumstances and concentrating on positives.

When I'm working with groups, given the chance I always ask the question "What makes a person successful?" Regardless of who I'm working with, there's always a long list: confidence, happiness, focus, a positive attitude, great communication skills, a good work ethic, luck, charisma, consistency… The list goes on, but the results are always the same. When you look at the attributes of a successful person and break them down into zones, 10% will always focus on features which relate to the person's mind and intellect, 10% will be skills-based, and a whopping 80% will be attitude-based.

And that's great news because *you* decide your attitude, and it's your attitude that will pretty much determine your skill level, intelligence and ultimately how successful you are with your clinic. The right attitude will establish your discipline and your ability to follow through on what this book will teach you. Decide now to take action and commit to giving yourself, your family, and the people important to you, the life you all deserve.

Targeting Your Ideal Customers

If you're marketing to everyone, you're marketing to no one. It's one of the biggest mistakes clinics make, and it's so easily rectified. Fear plays a big part; the fear is by targeting a specific type of person, you're cutting down on the number of possible clients, and yet the truth is quite the opposite. Rather than use the blunderbuss approach to marketing, the more precise you are in your target client, the more money you can charge (and so make) and the easier things will become.

As an example, I heard about a nutritionist, who was struggling to niche down. When asked who her ideal client was she responded 'anyone that can eat', which may be true but was far too broad. She was asked again, who and what do you want to niche down to, so she responded 'children'. She was told that was still too broad and asked what is was about children that she really wanted to focus on. She answered 'lunchtime meals', which let's be honest is very, very, niche. She then wrote a book entitled <u>Not Just Sandwiches</u> and branded herself as The Lunchbox Doctor. A short time later, she received a phone call from the BBC saying that they'd been let down by the person who was coming into talk about child obesity and asking if she was free for the next 30 minutes, she responded yes, and after a quick brief and a count down 5,4,3,2,1 she was on the air with national coverage. The moral of the story? The BBC's research team had searched online for someone who was focused on children's nutrition and Jenny was found easily and appeared a true expert. Such is the power of niching!

You might be sitting there thinking 'Well that's okay for them but I do work with a lot of different people, and I don't want to alienate my current clients.' Believe me, you won't. Your current clients will continue to use you.

Your first step is to look at what makes you the most profit in your business. What areas can you claim to be an expert in? And you can have more than one, but as a maximum I'd say three personally. I've seen some individuals claim to be experts in ten different treatments, and it just looks like they're a jack of all trades. Obviously it's different if it's a large clinic but if you're small, try not to be all things to all people. For those of us who are focusing on positioning ourselves as an authority, your competitors' lack of niching is great news. Get in front of their potential or current clients with the strategies and tactics laid out in this book, and you'll take them to the cleaners!

Just one word of warning, though, on having a single niche sector. Should something happen outside of your control that negatively impacts on these clients, your income could disappear overnight. In the last recession, for example, companies who were solely concentrated on one sector, pretty much had their budgets disappear overnight and couldn't adapt quickly enough to keep the cash coming in.

So, where niching can be great, try to build up two or three different areas over time so that your clinic is somewhat protected.

Okay, so let's say you've decided on your area and on what you're offering; the next thing to do is to build avatars of your ideal client. For example, one of my clients has three areas they've decided to concentrate on, and they've chosen to focus on one of those particular clients first for all their marketing efforts. This is 40+ mums, with a disposable income, whose children have just gone off to university, who now have more time on their hands, and who are looking to build their confidence.

They've gone on to build a much more detailed avatar and with this information they've been able to develop specific marketing strategies to engage in a way that this potential client wants to be engaged with. Just depending on who you're targeting, your own avatar should also be as detailed as possible, so consider where they live, what gender, age, children, where they holiday, what magazines they read, what social media platforms they're on… Really find out what they care about. Last year I interviewed Richard Reed from Innocent drinks (if you ever have the chance to visit Innocent HQ, take it; they're an excellent business with a really good fun culture). Anyway, when Innocent had reached a critical size, the next step was to approach the big four supermarkets in the UK. They were looking to approach just the buyers from these supermarkets, so they set about finding the names, and everything they could about these people – their interests, where they lived and, interestingly, how they got to work.

What they did next was genius. They didn't have the budget for mass-scale marketing so they simply sourced and paid for a handful of billboard advertisements for Innocent Drinks in and around the Tube stations these people used on their commute to work. To the buyers, it looked like Innocent Drinks were 'everywhere' and within a month they'd successfully booked meetings with them all. It might be that you can't employ that exact tactic but it demonstrates how knowing who your target market is allows you to direct your marketing efforts at them.

Your next step is to get your own marketing right. Your website and social media is basically your shop front; it's the first thing people will see when you either direct them to look at your services or they search for your services, so it's essential that you speak directly to them. Remember the e-commerce example earlier, so you need to alter your copy and website to be tailored to their very personal needs. The website needs to speak directly to your avatars.

Speaking of websites, there are only two jobs that a website should have, either to sell stuff so it's an e-commerce website, or to capture the details of people visiting the website. If it does neither of these tasks you're missing a trick and need to change it as soon as possible.

It's highly unlikely that as a clinic you're selling stuff online, so you're looking to somehow capture people's details through offering them some sort of download (often referred to as a lead magnet or in-bound marketing). If someone's on your website there is a really good chance that they're potentially looking to engage with someone offering your services. In exchange for a name and email address, or even an email address only (let's face it you can normally work out the name from the email address), you can offer them some advice and guidance; for example, 'Seven Questions You Must Ask' or 'The Three Most Common Mistakes That People Make When Choosing a Clinic.' The point of the download is to offer advice and guidance, not sell to the potential client by saying here at ABC we do X. It's about telling them the questions they should ask a clinic that will gently educate them about the advantages you offer your clients over the competition.

One question could be, "Do you give a guarantee on results?" then you explain why that question's important. Or you could say "If a clinic is unwilling to give guarantees then you have to wonder if they will be able to deliver what they're promising." The idea is for you to explain to the client what to look for when choosing a clinic and the pitfalls to avoid so they can make the best choice – which will hopefully be you. If you go to **www.TheBeautifulBusinessBook.com** there is an example guide for business coaches that I use on my website which should give you a flavour of the sort of thing you should be doing.

You could probably do a few different types of lead magnet or white papers, so that no matter what the person on your website is looking for you'll have a guide that will help advise and coach them. Also, make sure that you have a lead magnet on every single web page. I was speaking to a web design agency that had tracked all the visitors to different websites they'd designed with no lead magnets, and what they found the visitors were all doing (and they all did pretty much the same thing), was they'd hit the Home page, then look at the About Us, then the Contact page, before leaving without taking any action. If nothing else have something on your contact page for them to download as well as a last ditch effort to get their details.

Make sure as well that you have some strong photos of you and your team. As humans we're pre-programmed to look at faces, and we want to see who we'll be working with, so have videos there too which give an insight into who you are and your culture, and give people the opportunity to see you and connect with you in every way possible. Again think about who your avatar is with all of this. My partner's website is full of personality and pretty funky which is very deliberate as those are the sort of clients she wants to attract. If you were boring and a bit square, you'd probably wouldn't like it, but that's okay because you probably wouldn't get on with the business anyway, so making sure your values and personality shine through your website is a great pre-qualifier.

Next, think about the services you're targeting. You have a couple of choices about which landing pages you direct people to, so, on your website you can have dedicated pages where you have a page specifically for a service, but have it set up like a home page (so slightly more context-rich with a couple of lead magnets for people to download).

The other option is to have a satellite website which is where you have an exact design copy of your general website but change the content so that it is specifically tailored for each core service with its own appropriate URL and you can then drive your potential service-centric clients to that website. It shouldn't cost too much as the web designer is just copying the original website template, then placing different copy and pictures on there. The only potential downside of this tactic is that if a client then finds out that you do other services, it might be seen that you're not 100% transparent or that you're being a little sneaky, but only a bit.

Okay, so let's say you've got an all-singing-all-dancing website, now what? You have to drive traffic to your website and there are a number of options to achieve this. You could get someone to perform some Search Engine Optimisation (SEO) to get you to the top of Google through organic ranking, although as soon as the algorithms change you may drop or disappear so this shouldn't be relied on as your only strategy.

Another way might be through Google ads, as they can be a great way of driving specific traffic that is searching for your type of services to your website, although it can also be a minefield, so do take care. Google ad words have become extremely complicated over the past decade and it's very easy to waste money; in fact it's estimated that Google ads take $16 billion a quarter, with some claiming that $12 billion of this is utterly wasted because people have no idea how to set them up properly or to send traffic to appropriate landing pages. This is why in some quarters it's known as 'Google's stupidity tax.'

Be warned that if you're thinking of hiring somebody to

actually do the job for you, the truth is that many of the so-called Google ads experts aren't, and will throw your money away for you. I'm lucky enough to know somebody who is a real expert when it comes to Google ads, and he's been asked to look at people's Google ad accounts to check they were okay. Set up by so-called experts in their field, one particular account had two people working on it and when David checked they had only five negative keywords built into the search terms. Five!

Just in case this doesn't fill you with instant horror, or you don't yet know what a negative keyword is, it's a word which – if it comes up in the search that somebody's doing – ensures your advert won't be shown. You use it to when you're not interested in a specific market or niche, for example. So, if someone was looking for 'free treatments', as a clinic you're more than likely to be more interested in putting your advert in front of someone with some budget so this may be a negative word that you'd choose. We should all expect to start off with a few hundred negative keyword terms as a minimum, and experts like David build up many, many more. Over the last five years he's built up 5000 negative keywords for his own business and it's the primary driver of significant (and very cost-effectively-acquired) business for him.

There's too much to go into all of the Google ad words stuff in this book, so, as part of your free bonus, if you go to **www.TheBeautifulBusinessBook.com** you'll get a guide on the questions to ask your Google ads expert. Even if you decide to start off doing it yourself, this should still really help you consider what you need to do.

Social media is another way of driving traffic to your website, and one tactic that you may choose to use is the production of regular blogs, which you can then tweet about, and post on LinkedIn for people to see. This will also help your organic SEO, as Google likes to see credible links back to your website. When writing blogs, remember to think about the specific questions that your clients will be asking, as it's those questions that they will be Googling and which you need to include and answer.

Currently Facebook ads are a great way for clinics to engage with your potential avatars. With Facebook ads you can target based on gender, age, geographical area, and interests, which really allows you to specifically target the exact avatar you're looking for. And when thinking about the landing page you're pointing these ads to, make sure that the copy speaks directly to your potential client, and that there is some sort of download for people to take in exchange for giving you their email address. After all, it's a big ask to get people to pick up the phone and call you, but they'll be much more willing to give an email address where you can contact them if you tempt them with something of perceived value.

It's also worth mentioning that recent changes to Facebook mean that just because you have 100 likes on your Facebook page, when you post on the page, only about 5% of the people who like your page will actually see your post. This is because Facebook wants you to pay to get in front of people. Also, further recent changes to the rules means that when you're running competitions, if you ask people to like and share a page to enter the competition, and somebody complains about the fact you're asking them to share your page to join the competition, Facebook will shut your business page down. Again this is because they want you to pay to get your likes. The rules are ever-changing though, so do check them out regularly to avoid being caught out.

Just on social media, if you're going to do it make sure that you do it all the time – there's nothing worse than looking on the website and seeing that they haven't been blogging much recently. Even worse is when an clinic has a social media feed on their website and they haven't tweeted for a couple of months. It gives an incredibly bad impression and I guarantee that it will lose you credibility and prospects.

Also, set up searches across your social media platforms for your business name and your own name to regularly monitor what's being said about you, and remember that time moves quicker online and people expect a response within a far shorter timeframe than in the real world.

As well as blog, you should also be using video. YouTube is owned by Google and is the second largest search engine on the internet, so its importance will only grow from a search engine perspective. Statistically, short videos are more likely to get watched than an email is to be read, so videos are a very good way of communicating with your target market. If you really want to improve your SEO, using your blogs and sharing the video of the blog alongside the written content is a strong tactic.

Talking of online videos, there's a brilliant TED talk by Simon Sinek called "Why Great Leaders Inspire Action". If you've never seen TED it's a great resource of snappy 18 minute or so talks about pretty much any inspiring and educational topics you can think of. Their tag line is "ideas worth spreading" and it's definitely worth a look, no matter what your interests are. Anyway, we're going to cover in a later chapter the importance of your clinic's vision, mission, and culture, but understanding these things along with why you're in business can have a huge impact on your marketing.

In Simon's talk he talks about the Golden Circle in which you have three concentric circles, the centre, the middle and the outside. On the outside you have 'what you do', in the middle 'how you do it', and finally 'why you do it' in the inner circle which is your core purpose or belief as a business. Simon explained that all really inspired companies work from the inside out, rather than the traditional model where they work from the outside in, and he gave Apple as a great example.

If Apple was to market itself in the traditional way it would start with 'what it does' which would be something like "we make great computers", and then move on to "we make computers that are user-friendly, beautifully-designed and easy to use, want to buy one?" Now, what Apple actually does is start with their 'why', so their marketing message sounds more like "everything we do, we believe in challenging the status quo, we believe in thinking differently" before they move into the 'how', "the way we challenge the status quo is that everything we do is user-friendly, beautifully-designed, and easy to use", and then finally moving on to the what which is "we just happen to make great computers, want to buy one?".

He makes the point that people don't buy 'what' you do but 'why' you do it, and Jim Collins, the renowned author of <u>Good to Great, Great by Choice</u> and <u>Built to Last</u> made a similar point. He studied some of the top companies in the world and compared them to similar businesses within their respective marketplace, who had the same opportunities, but who failed to thrive, do as well, or who – in some cases – actually went out of business.

Jim found that all of the companies that did exceptionally well had a clear vision of what they were doing (their why), a mission statement, and a really strong culture that all of the staff and customers (even if they didn't fully understand it) took on in terms of what they were trying to achieve.

Now, I'm not saying that you have to be building a £multi-million company, but what I am saying is that people buy people, so knowing your 'why' will help your potential customers chose to buy from you.

Also, it's worth remembering that your current ideal clients that you're dealing with will have friends, family, and contacts that will also be your ideal clients, because birds of a feather flock together, so it's important you have some sort of strategy to ask for or get the contact details of these people too.

One extremely effective way is to run some sort of competition. For example, one of the clinics I'm working with decided to use a tombola to get referrals. They spent £2000 on prizes so there were a couple of good ones in there including tablets, a weekend away, and some really nice meals out, plus lots of little prizes to bring the total number up to 250. In exchange for two referrals which gave a specific name, telephone number, and email address, the person could pull one prize out of the tombola. The cost per lead of a potential new client worked out as just £4.00 here, which when you consider the potential lifetime value of a new client was massively good value.

Becoming a Must-Visit Clinic

Position yourself as the go-to person or clinic and make sure that people see this. Consider what accreditations are used within your industry, or what other accreditations could you get to differentiate yourself from the competition. They may even not mean that much to you, but your potential clients will see it as an example of how much more professional or just plain better you are than your competitors because you have them.

We've already talked about lead magnets, and how important it is for you to use them as a way of capturing people's data, so that you can then communicate with them, position yourself as the go-to person and ultimately – when they're ready to purchase – it's you they think of. You could also use white papers and other types of guides too though, and don't worry about giving stuff away and thinking about the competition getting hold of them. Anything you're already doing is out there somewhere anyway – how much better to be the first to give it to your potential client, and they'll think of you before anyone else.

Blog at least once a week and when thinking about your blog try to think about the questions people might be asking regarding your industry; it can also be a useful resource to send to potential and existing clients to again position yourself as the expert. Remember, you can also tweet out your blog, post it on LinkedIn and share across any other channels, and of course your blog will have a lead magnet, along with all your social media icons and share buttons, so will give visitors every opportunity to interact with you. If it doesn't, this is a real missed opportunity, so add them now.

I recently saw an excellent example of positioning from a website designer after the client had come on board with them. They had a series of emails welcoming the client, introducing them to the team and counting down from six weeks to when they'd start the website design. As they had a two week window to do the website, they also pointed the client to some of the blogs they had written, one of which focused on the advantages of working with a professional web design company. Each of the countdown emails also reminded the client what content they needed to provide, so, for example, they'd say 'Hi John, only another 15 days before we start your website. By now you should have shared your copy with us so we can…' The whole email sequence was automated but personalised brilliantly, really informative, and positioned the firm perfectly.

Opinion-based articles (often called op-ed or opinion-led) or by-lined articles in magazines or other media are also a great way of raising your profile. These are thought leadership pieces where your expertise can be evidenced and you can be positioned as a credible leader within your industry by offering advice and guidance. Normally the headline would be controversial such as "The Death of …. ", while the body copy would be much more managed, and you should come down very definitely on a certain side of whatever it is you're talking about so that you're seen as a person with a definite opinion. Sitting on the fence is a not a position you want to adopt, nor is it one that you want to be seen to be adopting, as it's often perceived to be weak (and you can get splinters!)

Every industry has awards and there are plenty of differing business awards that you can enter yourself into. Some of these are national ones like the 'UK Top 50 Advisor' award I won recently, or else there will be more regional or sector-centric awards you can apply for. This is an excellent opportunity for you to differentiate yourself from the competition. It takes a little bit of time and effort to actually put these applications together, but not only is it a great way to stand out from the crowd, these events are a great night out for your team and a real morale booster. There is a specific formula for writing winning award entries so it can be easier – and more effective – sometimes to get a specialist to do it for you, but it's well worth the investment as being shortlisted, or a finalist, can be a great profile raiser for your clinic.

Writing an e-book can be another good differentiator and a great way to be seen as the expert in your sector, but an even better strategy can be to write a hard copy book and then self-publish it. These days it's a lot easier than it used to be, and you can use Amazon's print-on-demand services which mean you aren't required to bulk-order your books and fill your garage up with them. As far as positioning goes, a physical book that you can put into people's hands will greatly increase their perception of you as an expert in your sector, and in the earlier example of The Lunchbox Doctor you can see the dramatic affect it can have. If you have no idea of how to start writing a book there are plenty of books and even online courses to help you take the first step.

Speaking at events is another great way of getting in front of your potential clients and raising your profile, especially if you're a keynote speaker. Becoming a good speaker does require effort, though, and for this I'd recommend joining something like the Professional Speaking Association or Toastmasters and attending speaking courses, workshops and training. Also, becoming a keynote speaker can take time as you often have to become very well-known within the industry. The alternative is to throw a lot of money at it to get you in that position. However, what you can do to circumnavigate this slightly, once you're proficient at speaking and you've got your speech nailed (and this means getting honest opinions from people that can speak), is to arrange your own fringe events at your target industry's main events. These would normally be something like a three day conference, so the idea is that you gently highjack the main event by creating your own event one of the evenings. Invite VIPs and other people already attending the main event and offer a champagne reception or similar. It's an opportunity for people to network, and then you can offer a high-value 20 minute skills session to whet their appetite on whatever it is you can do for them. Remember as well to give something away, ideally something that you need to send to them. Those who are interested in that are more likely to be interested in working with you so it's another great pre-qualifier.

With your clinic, you should be possible to offer some guarantees, whether these are time based or service based. It doesn't have to be money back and don't make the Ts&Cs a mile long either. I know with some treatments it can be difficult as results can vary due to a large number of factors, however during your consultation with the client you can talk them through everything to get them to understand any potential pitfalls. I also realise that with some treatments there are regulatory requirements in terms of what you can and can't say, however try to offer some sort of peace of mind. Sure, you may get some claims against it, however the number of potential clients that you convert into paying clients because of the offer should far outweigh any potential downsides.

This reminds me of the story of a Canadian jewellers, who were at $500,000 turnover. They worked with a consultant and he was really pushing them to do something that scared them, as he recognised that word-of-mouth is a great way to market your business. What they actually did in the end was genius. Once somebody bought an item of jewellery, they told them that if they lost the jewellery, broke it, a stone fell out or any other type of damage occured, all they had to do was return to the shop and ask for a replacement. Hell, they didn't even need to bring a receipt with them as they were on the system! None of this was advertised in any of the literature they produced and the jewellers were naturally really fearful of having lots of claims. In fact they set aside

$50,000 to cover claims for the first year alone, but were shocked to discover that they actually only had $5,000 worth of claims in that time. Their offer was so good though, and their customers were so blown away by it that they spoke to their friends and family and raved about the firm. It was a few years ago now that I actually spoke to the consultant who'd encouraged them to take this course of action, but at the time I spoke to him the company was turning over $20 million a year.

Again, remember to include your guarantee in your advice and guidance in the 'questions to ask before you engage with' document as the expectation that your client should have when they're looking to engage someone from your industry. There's a good chance that your competitors won't have that guarantee.

So, let's say you've implemented all of these strategies, what else? Well, it isn't just about using them in isolation, you have to use them across all your marketing activities. Opinion-led articles or PR, for example, is a great way for clinics to generate clients. In my experience, whenever the clinics I've been involved with have had opinion led articles or really meaty pieces in local papers or lifestyle titles, they've had clients off the back of it. However PR agencies can be a bit hit and miss, so included in my download bonuses at **www.TheBeautifulBusinessBook.com** is a guide on questions to ask a PR agency before engaging with them, written by an agency that I trust implicitly.

Now your article might not actually get read by your potential client, so get some hard copies and send a potential client or prospect a magazine with a post-it note attached that you're on pages five and six and thought they might be interested in the article. Or photocopy the pages and send to them. You could also send it out on your newsletter or place it on your website – in fact, just make sure that you use it wherever you can.

A nice strategy to employ is to get any awards, opinion-led articles, press releases, guarantees and accreditations you have on display in your reception or meeting room. Then, ensure that no matter what time someone turns up for a meeting or briefing, they're always left for a couple of minutes. What happens is that they start looking around at all the pictures, award, and commendations, so – by the time they sit down with you – their perception is already that you're expert and very, very good.

Also you need to have 'your right to be there' absolutely nailed. Your right is when you first sit down, or at some point in the first meeting, you tell the client about you and your clinic. This would typically include the years of experience you have in the industry, your expertise, name-dropping clients that are appropriate and who would impress, as well as awards, accreditations, and recent publications you'd been in. You do this so the client completely understands why you have the right to sit in front of them and offer advice. In the client's head they should perceive you as an expert and so someone they should listen too.

Helping Your Clients Buy More and More Often

Don't be under any illusion, you must have a sales process and you must have sales scripts. To not have these will really impede your growth and your ability to hand over the job of sales to a sales person. Having neither of these will cost you dearly.

You probably haven't seen this equation: $D \times V + FS > R =$ Sale (yes I know that D&V in medical terms is normally diarrhoea and vomiting) It's actually from a change formula developed during the 60s for businesses and corporations that want to carry out institutional cultural changes, but was adapted for sales in the 80s.

With most clinics, no matter the sector, normally the people sitting in front of you are there for very emotive reasons. They either have to be there, or they're there because something has really been seriously bothering them. In a world that seems to push perfection, people are feeling more self-conscious than ever about their appearance, and this has a knock-on effect on their self confidence that can impact on every area of their life's so it's important to understand exactly why they've come to you.

The D is the dissatisfaction or pain the customer has, V is the vision of what they want, FS is the first steps to get them to buy and R is resistance, which will be typical objections that you get to buying.

The idea is that you talk to the customer about their dissatisfaction making that D as big as possible, really digging around to find out what it is that's paining them. Get as much detail as possible, and ask them how it feels to be in that situation. Normally you have to ask a question at least three times before you uncover their pain. Really drill down and get them to describe, in depth, how they feel and what it means to them personally – where you can, make sure that the descriptions are vivid and rich.

Then, start building the V vision and again make this huge. Ask them to describe their perfect situation. Really dig around, ask what that looks like, what personal impact it has on them, how it will feel, what that would do for them, what impact it would have on their life and family. Make the vision bold, rich, and real. The bigger you can make the D and V, the easier the sale will be. Now, this isn't about manipulating people, it's simply about helping them to buy.

The FS, or first steps, is all about making the sale as much of a no-brainer as you can. Think payment in instalments, offering a money-back guarantee, 30 day trial periods, reminding them about any other cast iron guarantees you have, in fact anything that you can do to get buy-in. Once your customers decide to buy a little, they're likely to go the whole way because they'll already have made the decision to buy from you, and as people like to feel that they've made the right decision, they'll look for evidence to support this.

There's a great book called <u>Yes! 50 Secrets from the Science of Persuasion</u> by Noah J. Goldstein, Steve J. Martin and Robert B. Cialdini, and it's got all sorts of interesting facts about persuasion and how getting small buy-ins from people could lead to much larger ones simply because people felt a connection and identified with the issue, campaign, or opportunity.

For one test, they quoted that the researchers knocked on 100 houses and asked if they could put a large placard in the front garden saying "kill your speed". Not surprisingly, only 17% of householders said yes, and the others gave a flat no. Then, in a neighbouring, similar street, researchers knocked on the door and asked people if they could put a small sticker in their window saying "kill your speed". A huge 76% said yes, and when, three days later, the researchers went back to the houses that had agreed to display the small stickers and asked if they'd now put a large placard in the front garden 53% of them said yes. That's more than triple the initial number of the neighbouring street.

The reasoning is that taking that small action changed very slightly how these people viewed themselves. That little sticker in the window showed that they were the sort of person who cared about their community, and who didn't want people speeding, so when asked if they could put the much larger sign in the front garden many more identified with it and felt comfortable to say yes. Knowing that now, think about how can you get people to buy-in to what you do, or spend just a little bit, because they'll then be much more likely to spend more with you later.

R is resistance and it's all about reducing the resistance that will come through common objections that you'll already have had. It's just about recognising what you most often come across and preparing for it. If it's about price, remind them of the value and the vision of what you're going to help them achieve, or if they want to delay, remind them of the repercussions of that and repeat back to them what you found out when talking about their pain or dissatisfaction.

It might be that you go through this and then the client wants to think about it. Again, remember to include your right within the information they take away, just to remind them of everything you've already covered. If they haven't already had it, include your guide on 'questions to ask before you engage with <our sector>' and remember to also include testimonials from existing clients. Also, try to stand out slightly, rather than just giving it to them, emailing the proposal over and send it over in a well packed brochure.

Make sure that you understand their concerns and how your clinic is the best fit. Include your right but make sure that your client understands the relevance to them. One of my clients won a customer against a much larger, more specialist business because the other guys presented 'their right' in the wrong way. They talked about 'we've done this' and 'we've done that' and 'we've won this'. When my client talked to her potential customer, she shared the credible background but went on to explain what it meant to them. So 'we've done this which means that you can benefit from…' The other business just came across as if they were bragging, and ultimately didn't win the customer's business.

If you've ever watched The Apprentice, where Alan Sugar seems to spend his time criticising and firing people, there's an excellent example of a presentation pitch done by Helen Miliband. In the presentation they were trying to sell a child seat to a French company, and one of the directors came up with a price objection saying the seat is too expensive. Helen's partner in the pitch then took the seat and sat on it, saying 'how comfortable it was' which just makes you cringe as you watch. She's completely ignored the objection and has made a pointless comment.

Helen took control of the situation though – thankfully – and pointed out that modern women these days will pay almost anything for convenience, that she'd studied their target market, and that the price is a reasonable one considering how much convenience this gives them. Plus, she told them, they could say they were the first people to bring this to France and that they care about their customers, care about their children's safety, know how busy their customers are and that this is a great product for them. Needless to say, Helen won the pitch. If you want to see it, search for Helen's sales pitch The Apprentice on YouTube, and enjoy. It's a really great example of knowing what buttons to press because you understand and know who your customers are.

Now, spoiler alert here, if you ever go and see Brad Sugars speak live, he normally tells this story. He'd taken on a client who sold tyres. When he asked what his conversion rate was on the calls his sales team were getting, the owner guessed at about 70%. Brad asked him to monitor it for two weeks, just to double-check what it actually was.

Two weeks later Brad came back and the owner was fuming – he was actually only getting 17% conversion on the calls! Brad focused on getting the sales team to work up a simple script, something they could use when someone called, it went something like this: "Before I give you a price would it be okay to ask a couple of questions?" The customers always say yes. "Can I ask what kind of driving you do? Is it long distance or short? Is it motorway or country roads? Do you have your family in the car or are you driving on your own? Do you drive fast or slow?"

At the end they'd say "Based on your driving habits the safest and most economical tyre for you would be XXXXX." "We have a space this afternoon so if you can make that we can do you a special deal of £XX." If the person couldn't make it, they'd always ask if they could hold that deal till they could get there and the salesperson would say, "Of course; I just need your credit card details to take the payment now."

The conversion tripled to 49% using that script, and what it does is change the conversation from price, to the safest and most economical. The questions reminded the person about the importance of the tyres on their car and the salesperson was acting as more of a consultant and being perceived as an expert who was there to help them. Best of all they used an internal reference for the tyres to avoid customers simply price-matching elsewhere. A very smart move.

The same has to be true of any clinic. You have to ask questions to find out what the client's end goal is, then advise them on the best fit to get them there. You need to be a consultant, not a sales person. I worked with a clinic that adopted this and it had a huge impact on their bottom line. A lot of their clients were very price sensitive and would come in with a particular budget in mind, however when they talked to them about what they were actually trying to achieve, they were able to bolt on other treatments to help the client achieve their goals.

Remember, if your client has a budget of £3,500 and you want to get a £4,000 sale, you're only selling an extra £500, so you can talk about the £500, not the £4,000. You can even break it down to the lifetime cost that it's worth to them. I once saw someone selling membership for an organisation; the annual cost was just under £1200 at £99 a month. A woman in the group commented that they thought that was a bit expensive but when, a minute later, the presenter likened the membership to purchasing a Starbucks coffee every day, the same person then commented on how cheap it was. Same deal, just presented another way.

I did something similar myself a few years back when I wanted to take my daughter Ellie to Lapland. It was a five-day all-inclusive trip with activities every day. You basically spent every day looking for Santa with a bus driving you around to different locations each day. At every location one of the four lead elves would entertain the children, there'd be some kind of building such as Santa's post office, where the elves slept, and toy-making workshops, and there'd be activities such as dog sleighs, reindeer rides, and snowmobiles. All of which was building up to the final day when the youngsters would eventually meet the man himself.

The trip was going cost nearly £4000 and at the time money was tight but I decided to do it anyway. I looked at the lifetime value to my daughter and to me of these special memories, and broke them down so that they weren't costing me nearly £4000, they were costing just a few pence per day. It was such an incredibly magical trip that even when I think about it now, it makes me smile.

You may find yourself in a situation where you ask about a client's budget and the client gives you a firm answer. No matter what they say, make sure to add 'up to' and then shut up and don't say a word, just wait for their response. In many cases, the client will give you a much higher figure, and this gives you the opportunity to much more comprehensively answer the client's brief, to do a much better job for them, and of course plenty more opportunity to show your value. I do suggest quoting just under the maximum figure they give though. Just so they feel they're getting value for money.

We spoke earlier about the importance of building your list, so you're probably thinking 'great, what now?' For most clinics these will be high income people who are incredibly difficult to get in front of. It's not a problem though; it's all about how you contact them. You just have to turn up in a completely different way that makes you stand out and get a response, even if that response is telling you to clear off! In my experience, though, the worst case scenario is that you'll get a polite no from the very person you're targeting. There are a few strategies but some variety on lumpy mail always goes down well, or even a shock and awe package, let me explain…

Recently I've been interviewing some of the country's top business people for an NLP modelling project on the mind-set of the super successful. The idea is to find out what's happening on an unconscious level that makes these people really excel at business and to find out what the common traits among them are, as well as what they have in common that will be an important marker. Once we've learned all of this, essentially we have the business holy grail – a blueprint for success. The problem is these people don't know me, they get a barrage of requests for different things, are really time pressured and they have the ultimate gatekeepers whose sole job is not to let anyone near them. So how did I do it?

Well, as an example, I got myself invited to an Innocent Drinks event hosted at the company's HQ in London, and had the opportunity to talk to Richard Reed, one of the co-founders of the company. I explained about the modelling project I was working on and asked him if it would be okay to interview him. He said it sounded like a great idea but he was too busy and warmly wished me the best of luck.

Enter the shock and awe package. Richard had spoken that night about the need to be persistent in whatever you were trying to achieve and likened it to tapping on an egg. If you just kept going eventually 'the chick of yes' would pop out. So I got a chicken egg, emptied the contents, went to a local hobby store and bought a kit to make up a small Easter chick, which I had to glue together Blue Peter style, and hey presto, the chick of yes was hatched (actually, the way I glued it together it looked like a slightly deranged chick of yes).

I then commissioned a local artist to do a series of drawings showing how, if Richard took me up on my offer of a time management workshop for his team (in return for the interview), this would help his team sky-rocket their performance and give him more time. I put all this in a box along with the chick of yes and a few added-value items and a few days later I got a congratulatory email from Richard saying good effort and telling me to contact his PA and make an appointment for the interview.

I've approached a lot of truly successful big name business owners and I always follow up and always get a response from the person in question, even if it is a no. I try to find out something about them and then personalise what I'm sending; for example, Theo Paphitis mentioned in an article he liked marmalade on a Saturday morning, so I sent him an award-winning jar. He said no but that's still a response. He's actually had two now, so I've had two nos but I always find persistence is important in business and I'm going to get my mum to make a jar up and send it to him – hopefully that will get a yes; who can refuse a mum?☺

Kelly Hoppen mentioned in another publication that she really liked white marshmallows and would get a bag of the mixed ones and pick out the pink ones and throw them away, so I sent her a bag that had hardly any pink ones in them. I followed up with a phone call and her PA (who was lovely) explained that she was too busy but liked the marshmallows. Just recently I found and sent some award-winning vanilla ones and I again followed up with a phone call – as soon as I mentioned to the PA what I sent in the post she exclaimed 'Oh they were delicious; you're in my pile of people to contact, can I call you later this week?' and that was a few days ago, so fingers crossed I can get my interview with Kelly now.

If I can touch some of the hardest-to-reach people in the country using this method, you can get in front of your dream clients. Anyway, even if you're sending a KitKat and tea bag offering them the chance to 'take a break', they're far more likely to engage with whatever it is you are sending them. But, and here's the pitfall for many, just because you've sent them something, don't expect them to ring you, you absolutely need to follow up, also try to drive them to do something online, then you can see if they're interested, preferably with a phone call if you can, maybe an email checking that the box got through or even something prior to you sending the package just to say "something's on its way to you", to create a little intrigue. The main thing is to have some steps in place and to follow up on the phone with further follow-ups planned for if you don't get through to them initially. Remember the life-time value of these clients, what would you be prepared to pay to get them as clients?

Just while we're thinking about sales, are you going to buy a car today? This year? In the next three years? How about the next five years? Chances are if you didn't say yes to any of the others, you definitely said yes to that last one, and it will be the same for your potential clients. They might not be buying today but they will be at some point, and your job is to stay in front of them so that when they do buy you're front of mind to contact. So, stay in touch with them, and make sure that you link with them on all the social media platforms they're on too.

You might from time to time choose to take a stand at some events – they're a great way of raising your profile. Don't make the mistake of just turning up and setting up a stand though, remember you're looking to make contact with people and collect data, so always try and have some sort of competition, even something as simple as asking people to fill out the form to enter a draw. Have more recent guides or white papers you can give away, but again actually send them a pack and capture all of their details.

There may even be an opportunity to do some more detailed targeting. I heard about a business recently who was going to be at trade event and did something quite clever. They contacted the organisers and asked them for a list of contact details for the booked attendees, and while the organisers wouldn't give them out, they did share the names of the firms that were going there. It was a little more work, but the business contacted each of the firms to ask who was going to the trade event, then – having gotten the name – rang the person and asked them what their favourite chocolate bar was. They promised that, no matter how bizarre the request, this would be waiting for them on their stand at the trade event so to come along to collect it.

They actually upgraded the packages to include a nice bottle of wine in a presentation box, and on the first day of the event so many people crowded round the businesses stand to pick up their chocolate (and their wine) that it created a huge buzz (as well as lots of goodwill). The result of this work?

They made £tens of thousands worth of sales at and soon after the event, and developed some string relationships for future sales too. It's examples like this that just go to show it's the hard work upfront that makes the selling easy.

You could do something similar in an offer for people attending the event you were at, get them to fill something out prior to attending and then make sure they have something to pick up from your stand.

Lastly, and this does sound a bit obvious, but it's still estimated that 80% of sales are lost because nobody asks for the sale. Just make sure that you have a way of asking for yours. I spoke with a prospective client a few years ago and they mentioned that they were doing a big pitch for a job they wanted. When I bumped into them again I asked them how they got on, and they said 'great, I left them to think about it…' When I dug down, what appears to have happened is that they delivered a great 45 minute pitch for their product and at the end told the client to think about it, because they were too scared to ask for the sale in case they said no. Just make sure that you don't fall into the same trap and that you have a way of asking the sale that you're comfortable with – even if it's something like 'do you wanna give it a go?'

Developing Perfect Pricing

I'm going to be slightly challenging here and suggest that chances are the only reason you're not charging more for your services are the six inches between your ears. The amount of businesses I go into that don't charge what they're worth is shocking. Yes, you need to do some of the positioning and sales process stuff that we've talked about in the previous chapters, but on the whole, if you were talking to your dream clients you could almost instantly put up your prices, but probably won't through fear.

Fear of losing your existing clients, fear of them telling you you're too expensive, fear of money not coming in, losing your business, your house, losing your team, fear that your clinic isn't good enough. All of this is in your head and it's one of the biggest challenges that a lot of clinics face. On the flip side, I do come across the odd clinic that's charging lots and, to be honest, they often suck at what they do, so how come they're able to charge so much?

Again, it's down to the six inches between the ears of the

person leading the clinic and the perception that gives potential clients. If they're charging double what you are they have to be twice as good, right? Not always the case, and remember some clients won't know what great service is, so they'll just assume what they're getting is as good as it gets (remember I talked about giving advice and guidance to help your potential clients understand what good and bad is).

It's also worth having this as part of your sales process. I've had one clinic, for example, who sometimes come across challenges in pricing with clients. Here it's worth reminding the client what they're ultimately searching for. Say the client wants to look younger, it's worth digging around to find out why. It might be that they're recently single, not feeling that confident (dissatisfaction) and by feeling younger they're sure they'll have more confidence, will talk to more people, more naturally, and hopefully meet Mr or Mrs Right (vision). Again, you should be positioning yourself here as a consultant and helping them get the best match for what they are trying to achieve. Show them that they're in safe hands with you because of (insert your right) and the price you're asking them to pay is more than worth it.

The second thing that helped my client put up their prices was a change in the clients they were looking to work with. Once their avatars were built and they started to actually think about the value they were delivering to these clients that had the budget, the price increases became a no-brainer. Actually, even before they had a chance to really start targeting the clients they had selected, clients with the budget they were looking for started to turn up. Not sure if that's law of attraction but it's not a fluke, as I've seen this happen time and time again. Over the last 18 months, they've doubled their prices and I think they have room to potentially double them again, especially having seen the results of some larger, more prestigious clinics that are charging well above what they are delivering. On top of this, when approaching these top-end clients if the price was too low, they wouldn't see value for money, and they'd just assume that you weren't that good.

And price perception is key. A recent story showed that the majority of people can't tell the difference between expensive and cheap bottles of wine. In an episode of 'Observatory' on the hit YouTube channel 'Vox', 100 people tasted three bottles of wine priced at $8, $14 and $43 respectively. After a series of questions, tasters rated the least expensive and the most expensive exactly the same. Which begs the question, what's the point in buying expensive wine when, taste-wise, you're likely to get a similar experience to cheaper alternatives? In all honesty, it comes down to (and always will come down to) who you're selling to. Your 'market', and their perception of what quality is. Because, naturally, peak prices denote quality to most people, and there is a market that will always buy into that; who will buy into the status that comes with buying expensive, no matter what the product.

While we're talking about pricing it's well worth mentioning cash flow. It's all about reducing your risks and keeping the money flowing. If you can get people on to some sort of retainer then it's well worth thinking about setting up a direct debit to better manage and control your cash flow. But you do need to ensure it's always win-win (for you, and the client).

One strategy I'm seeing a number of clinics employ to great success is a VIP membership. The idea here is that you target your very best clients, and put on a VIP membership launch day where you invite them along and treat them to some champagne and nibbles, before announcing your new VIP membership and all its benefits. Remember, this is a limited number of places only and because these people are your very best clients you are offering it to them first.

Make it a bit of a no-brainer, so if it's costing £150 a month, give them RRP £200 worth of treatments, make it a rolling 12 month contract and make sure that you make them feel special. Even if you only have 20 people in your VIP membership, that means on the first of every month you'll have £3,000 drop into your bank which should take the pressure off having to start from zero each month.

You may even be able to offer your clients better terms for up-front payments. I had one client where I suggested that they offer a pre-pay deal where, if the client paid three months up front for a year, they'd get month 13 for free. This had two benefits – firstly, it was increasing their cash flow, and secondly it was helping to tie clients in for twelve months so that they'd get month thirteen for free. Initially the client was really resistant, quoting industry best practice and a number of other excuses, but once they ran out of excuses and tried it, a number of clients took the offer up and it flipped their cash flow overnight.

If you're unsure about your pricing, take a look at your much bigger competitors or even those of a similar size. Now, you do have to compare apples with apples, but looking at their delivery, how far away are you from them? Do you really understand your marketplace? And are you constantly attending courses to evolve your knowledge and understanding of your industry best practice? To stay fresh? Do you understand the strategy behind what you're trying to do? If so, you'll absolutely wipe the floor with the majority of your competitors.

Also, if your client comes back and says your pricing is a bit on the high side, ask them what they think their budget could stretch to. I'd never suggest reducing your price but you could offer to 'part fund' the first three months of the treatment to show the value that you bring (remember FS from your sales equation). This is also known as their puppy dog sales tactic, so, someone comes into a pet shop because they've been dragged in there by the kids and the kids are pestering for a puppy. The pet shop owners says take the puppy for the weekend, the kids will be fed up of looking after it by the end of the weekend and be back on their Xbox, which they are, but by then the parents (the decision makers) absolutely love the puppy and wouldn't part with it, so return to the pet shop, buy the puppy and a load of other stuff that's needed for looking after it. What's your puppy?

One last thing on pricing; have you noticed that the clients that push you down on price are a bigger pain in the arse and typically take more of your time than any other client? It's often questionable if you actually make any money from them. Plus, while you're spending all your time looking after them you're ignoring your well-paying clients that take a fraction of your time. They may be sitting there feeling unappreciated and thinking of leaving you (68% of lost clients go because they thought you didn't care). I bet when you took on these people that just drain you resources, you had a gut feeling that they were going to bit difficult but decided to ignore it and thought it would be okay.

Do yourself a favour, and if you can't educate them into understanding how great you are and what they need to do to make this a win-win partnership, ditch them and give them to your competitors. You'll feel better, you'll have more time to grow your business with the clients you want, and you'll feel good about that too.

And if potential clients not turning up to appointments is an issue for you, it's really important that you get a deposit for two reasons. Firstly, if somebody pays a deposit no matter what the amount, they're much more likely to turn up. Once they've let you down it will be almost impossible to get hold of them because they'll feel guilty and so won't want to talk to you. And secondly it's important that you value your time and if somebody is going to let you down they still need to pay something.

Getting Your Clinic to Run Without You

Understanding the flow of work and tracking it are absolutely essential for any clinic, as are getting the team to understand the commerciality of what they're doing. After all, if they save 30 minutes each working day, over a year that will result in an extra two working weeks of time that can be filled with treatments!

Within any clinic you need to have dedicated roles, sometimes you can start to get cross overs, or people helping people out because it's a five minute job for them to do it, but over time this will really start to hurt productivity so you have to keep people within the boundaries of their job. Also, play to people's strengths. It's not always obvious where people will really excel, so talking to your team and asking what they see their role becoming or if there's anything they feel they'd prefer doing is well worth the conversation.

Give people ownership of certain clients or treatments as well. This will cut down on confusion from the clients side if they only deal with one or two people at most, it will also help the team member get a real feel for that treatment and enable them to become a real expert a lot quicker than if they were covering a few treatments or differing clients, thereby getting them to deliver better results more consistently.

Giving ownership will also empower the team to do better. Being micro-managed has been shown to be detrimental to productivity, so when you delegate jobs be sure to tell your team members what the end result should look and feel like, then let them get on with it so that it also becomes a learning opportunity for them. This is by far one of the best ways of developing your team. There may be a few mistakes along the way, (non-treatment type) but as the saying goes, people who don't make mistakes don't do anything. Make sure, along with the ownership, you give them deadlines, and try and let them manage their own time.

If you've only just started to grow your team, the one big lesson you have to learn – and fast – is that in a lot of cases, you're probably really great at what you do and the people you bring on aren't going to be as good as you at first. You'll be tempted to either micro-manage things or, in some of the cases I've seen, even tempted to shrink your clinic again. Don't! You have to let go and concentrate on putting systems in place to maintain high standards of delivery across the clinic. Look to get rid of all the jobs you're doing – ultimately you want your business to be a commercial profitable enterprise that keeps paying you even if you walk away from it, don't you?

Make sure, as well, that your customer relationship management system (CRM) is completely up-to-date and being utilised fully. There are a variety of CRMs available; you can get industry-specific ones or more general ones, just make sure that every person that contacts you goes on to your CRM along with where they heard of you, and as much information as you can possibly get. You can then tag these people so that, when you have to, you can retrieve them and send them relevant information that they will find of interest.

When choosing a CRM make sure that you understand everything that you want it to do. We referenced a web design agency's automated CRM as a great example earlier, but this is sophisticated and not many CRMs can fully handle this type of functionality, so if it's something you'd like to replicate make sure to check your preferred system has the capability.
Ideally put together a shopping list of items that you want your CRM to do before committing to one. Most systems will give you a free trial so you can try before you buy. Remember that all your future wealth is in your database so do make sure you keep it up-to-date and relevant.

I'd also recommend using a CRM that will either integrate with your online diaries or provide it's own online diary system for everything that you do within your clinic, including bookings, holidays, and training courses. Whatever you do, don't have multiple diaries, get everyone using a single system. Google Calendar is excellent for this purpose and I can highly recommend it.

Also ensure that what you're focused on within the business is the one thing that will make you the most money. We mentioned Steve Jobs earlier and how when he returned to Apple he reduced the amount of products Apple was producing to actually turn Apple around.

It's worth talking about his mindset and how he used this principle for when he joined Pixar after being ousted from Apple. Pixar was supplying computers to the movie industry that created the CGI and cartoons; Jobs saw that these computers were selling for a few $tens of thousands but they were producing films that grossed $tens of millions.

He saw that to make real money he needed to take Pixar into the movie-making game, and how he went about it was absolutely brilliant. Jobs approached Michael Eisner, the then CEO of Disney, and told him what he was going to do. He proposed that they would do a joint venture with Disney to produce a new cartoon with new characters (now remember, at this point Disney hadn't produced a new cartoon character for ten years and were struggling, but they were still Disney and had never collaborated).

Jobs proposed that Pixar and Disney partner on this new cartoon and Eisner recognised that this could be the shot in the arm that Disney needed. But then Jobs told him that he wanted 50-50 share on the credits for the film. Eisner flatly refused; Disney had been around forever, their credibility was massive, they were a household name, and Pixar was a complete unknown! Now, what Jobs was doing here was very clever, it's something called up-branding. By aligning Pixar with Disney on a 50-50 basis, Pixar would become a big name in the movies instantly.

Jobs said it was 50-50 on the credits or he'd walk away, and Eisner was ultimately worried enough that another studio would take Jobs up on his offer that he eventually agreed to the deal. The first film was Toy Story and it was a massive hit. Fast forward to Jobs re-joining Apple, and remember I said that he had to sell Pixar; well, he sold it to Disney for $7 billion! One of the main reasons it was worth so much was that Disney had originally up-branded Pixar with its name.

Within your business everything needs to be systemised, and this is quite a daunting job when you think about all the different activities that your clinic undertakes. In fact it's quite often the one thing that gets left as the immediate benefits aren't clear, but having systems is absolutely essential if you want to be in a position where you can walk away from your business and it will keep running without you, or if you want to sell it.

Some time ago I was doing some investigative positioning research, ringing round a variety of different businesses to learn more about their pricing structure, posing as a potential client that wanted some work done. Out of 10 businesses I phoned, only one asked my name, email address and phone number. One, out of ten. And I started by explaining that I was a prospect. Even this one business failed to follow up on my phone call though, or stay in touch with me using their monthly newsletters. What a huge failure in their systems, but what a great learning for us. Whoever is answering the phone in your clinic should have a script to work with and know exactly what to do in certain situations. Ultimately, if a potential client calls, at the very least they should take a name and phone number, add them immediately onto your CRM and attach the appropriate tags, and get an appropriate person to call them back – promptly.

And why stop there – every part of your clinic should be systemised. Start by getting your team together and make a list of every single task that is done. Agree on a format for writing out these tasks and then delegate each out amongst your team. Once all of these are written out, you should be able to produce a flow diagram for each task, with each box relating to a certain page in your supportive folder. And don't hesitate to use resources like Elance to outsource the production of the diagrams – it's about using your time most effectively, so make the call.

To make things easy for you I've an example task and related flow diagram as one of the free downloads available to you at **www.TheBeautifulBusinessBook.com**.

Making Your Clinic the Best Place to Work

Your vision and mission for the business, and the culture that you're looking to develop or maintain, needs to be written down for everyone involved with your business to see. And the power of this shouldn't be minimised. In <u>Delivering Happiness,</u> Tony Hsieh shares the story of how he sold his first company for $250,000,000 and tells how in the early days he was excited to go into work, he loved the people he was working with, and was having a great time. In the early days he was offered $2,000,000 for the company but held onto it, not because it wasn't a lot of money, but because he loved what he was doing. However, as the company grew, Tony lost the joy and eventually – just before he sold the company – he really had to drag himself into work. At first he struggled to understand why he felt like that, but when he was in work one day and looking around, he realised that the place just felt a lot different – it had grown quickly and the new people coming into the business had different attitudes and ways of doing things.

The business that Tony loved had now developed a culture and values of its own, and they were at odds with what Tony and his partners had first set up. And this meant that he no longer felt like he belonged there, nor did he want to be there. So, Tony promised himself that the next business he was involved with would not suffer the same issues. And when he did get involved with Zappos, he worked with his team to develop a collaborative written vision, mission, and values for the company. Anyone coming into the business was shown these and it was made clear that they had to fully engage with the company's culture.

Now this is powerful stuff, and I can wholeheartedly recommend that you consider it in your business if you don't have it already. It's been well documented that if people verbalise a belief, even if it's one that they didn't hold before, they are much more likely to act as if that belief is real. Even if you're sitting there thinking 'my business has already developed a culture that I don't like' you have the power to change it.

It's a bit of an old cliché saying that your greatest asset is your people, and it's said that a happy workforce is a productive workforce. Well, the Department of Economics at the University of Warwick carried out some research and demonstrated that happier people were actually 12% more productive, they were able to work quicker and without a drop off in quality.

The best place to work philosophy is all about asking your team 'If this was absolutely the best place to work, what would it look like?' Then you can start to build up a picture to work towards. It's different for every clinic because of the team that you've recruited and culture you've built, but you might be surprised at how easy and cost-effective implementing some of the requests are, and what a huge difference to morale and the feel of the clinic they bring.

In <u>The Happiness Advantage</u> by Shaun Achor, he cites an experiment which saw doctors given patients' notes of symptoms and past medical history to diagnose what was wrong with them now. Simple enough, but doctors have to be creative in their problem solving when diagnosing, as inflexibility in thinking has been shown to be a major cause of misdiagnosis (doctors can get stuck in a rut and won't question the first assumptions in diagnosing a patient, even if there is overwhelming evidence against it).

So, they split doctors into three groups. One group was primed to be happy, the next given medical statements to read, and the last given nothing. The aim of the test was not to see how fast they came up with right diagnoses, but how if affected their ability to come up with the correct diagnosis. What they found was that the doctors primed to be happy correctly diagnosed the patients twice as fast as the control group, and were less likely to get stuck in a rut with their thinking, when compared with both other groups. Now that's a pretty impressive result!

You may be wondering how the doctors were primed to be happy. Were they given a big pay rise? A free holiday? A new car? No to all. They were actually given a piece of candy which they weren't even allowed to eat until later, in case the sugar rush somehow affected the results. Just imagine the power of that in your clinic.

Another brilliant example of how you can steer the culture of a business and benefit from the hugely positive impact on the people in it is Seattle's Pike Place Fish Market, which is now world-famous. Read the short book <u>Fish</u> by Stephen C. Lundin, Harry Paul and John Christensen to learn more about how they achieved the culture they did, but it's a wildly successful, fun, and bustling place, with a joyful atmosphere and fantastic customer service. The team literally throw fish from one side of the market to the other, and they get crowds of people coming down to see the action and even get involved. However, it wasn't always that way, it used to be just a job to the employees and not a great one as it was often cold and smelly.

But they all came together one day and decided that if they were going to come to work every day they might as well be the best, and have fun doing it. Through a process of trial and error, they learnt by applying ingeniously simple lessons which allowed them to become The World Famous Pike Place – and it's interesting to note that they actually called themselves 'world famous' long before they actually were (remember what we were talking about earlier about beliefs…). They now have lots of fun, and you can do the same to energise and transform your workplace if you choose to.

So, having given you some evidence that investing a little effort in your team will yield positive results, what are some of the things that you can do? Well, you can start by actually asking your team what is it that they want and what they would like the clinic to be like in five years' time. This in itself will make you stand out and start getting engagement because so few employees are ever asked, but you do have to be seen to follow through.

One of the businesses I work with gives everyone their birthday off as an extra day's holiday – and it's compulsorily that they do something fun. The team also decided to have a book club, so every month when they have their team meeting people report on a book they've read that month, that's taken from library that the business has built up. They also have regular nights out, attending things like cookery training, as well as some more adventurous stuff, they've also got a Pinterest board set up for what the future office looks like (someone's even pinned a picture of a slide from the first floor to the ground floor), and there are plans for a long weekend to Barcelona when the agency hits certain targets. This works for them because it works for the team, but every business is different because every team is different.

Something that I'd highly recommending doing as well is finding out what personal goals your employees have, big and small – most people have no idea how to set goals properly or even that they should be writing them out. You can do this by getting someone in to run a goal-setting workshop, and during the process you should at some point be writing down a list of things that you would like to achieve. Get people to share their goals but, as the boss, ask if you can have a copy of everyone's just to help them to achieve them and to give them reminders from time to time.

The list actually gives you a real insight into how to reward your staff and make them feel valued. Sure, some of the stuff they've written down will be things like an Aston Martin

DB9 which might be slightly outside your remit to reward, but other stuff will be really easy like a balloon flight or going to the theatre. One agency employee I know of had always wanted a goldfish, so at the next event a large goldfish bowl was bought to collect people's business cards, and when they'd finished with it after the event, they gave it to her along with the fish itself.

Carrying out regular appraisals is critical for building a team that excels, and it has to be a two-way process. This is about finding out what they'd like in the way of support and training, and also allows you to set targets and expectations. It can feel like a time-consuming task but the effort is absolutely worth it. If you're not communicating with your team, and they're not exactly sure of what's expected of them, how can they grow? So you need to cover successes that have been achieved, share constructive criticism to help them improve if there have been any problems, and identify any skills needed and training that's required.

And just on feedback, it can be good for us, good for the people we work with and good for our employer. Constructive criticism helps us not only to improve our performance in the job we do now but also make decisions about the skills we need to develop in order to achieve our ambitions for our future career.

Building a Brilliant Business Plan

This may not be the largest section of the book but it is the most important bit. I see a lot of clinics that don't have a working business plan, and it's one of the most important parts of building a successful clinic.

Without a plan how can you possibly know what to focus on? Without a plan how can you avoid being a busy fool? You become someone who's working really hard with their head down, simply ploughing through stuff, and never looking up to see where they're going. All of which reminds me of a friend of mine called Johnny. Johnny comes from a farming background, and he was telling me how when he was a youngster his brother taught him to plough a field. He got him in the tractor and told him to concentrate on the front wheel and keep that in the furrow of what had already been done, which was a dead straight line. Johnny ran the full length of the field and when he got to the end, his brother told him to look behind him at what he'd ploughed.

Johnny turned and saw something that was about as far from a straight line as you could possibly get. So, his brother took over, straightened up the furrow and put Johnny back in the driver seat. This time he said "watch the wheel and keep it in the furrow but also pick a spot on the horizon directly in front and keep an eye on that". Again, Johnny ran the full length of the field, looking to the horizon and keeping an eye on the wheel in the furrow. This time, when he got to the end and turned around to look, he'd ploughed a perfectly straight line.

And that's how everything works. No matter what it is you're trying to achieve, you have to look to where you're going, as well as have an eye on what's going on now. I see too many clinic owners who not only don't have a plan for the now, but aren't really clear about where they're going either. And that's a bit like deciding to go on holiday, turning up to any old airport, pointing at an aeroplane and saying 'that one will do', and all without even having your passport or a suitcase. Actually, the average person probably spends more time planning their holidays than they do planning their life, which is clearly a completely crazy way of doing things!

Johnny went on to enjoy a high-powered career in the corporate world before starting his own consultancy, GOOD2GREAT, with his business partner Gary. They've shared a few tools with me for reference in this book so I wanted to take the opportunity to pass on my thanks.

Remember how earlier we talked about things being *important-and-urgent* and that what's *important* should never get sacrificed for what's *urgent*? Well, building your overall strategy and plan is super-important, I'd suggest that you read through the next few pages once or twice, and then set aside at least a few hours in your diary to work through the whole process. Treat this as an appointment with your most important client…You!

The next five steps are about developing a strategy and plan to really give you focus. I'd also suggest and that you involve others who have a vested interest in your business success. That could be business partners, your senior management, spouse or life partner; whoever is important to you. Ask them to challenge you and offer potential solutions.

	NOW	TWO YEARS	FIVE YEARS
B U S I N E S S			
L I F E S T Y L E			

Draw this out on a flip chart pad or on a large piece of paper. What is important is to really get an understanding of what lifestyle you want, so this is where you need to nail it down.

In five years' time what do you want your life to look like? Think about where you're living. What type of house do you have? How many bedrooms are there? How is it furnished? What does your garden look like? Do you have outbuildings? And pets? What about an orchard, a lake or a swimming pool?… You get the picture. Make this a really rich image and note *everything* down.

Now think about your working week. What does that look like? How many holidays are you taking? How are you getting there? And remember that this is in five years so you can set whatever target you want. How many long weekends are you taking and which destinations are you travelling to? What cars are you driving? What colour are they? What do the interiors look like? Do you have any other vehicles like a motorbike, jet ski, or track day car?

And what else is going on? Have you written a book? Do you have a property portfolio? Have you had children? Or maybe you're sending ones you already have to private school? Perhaps you've learnt to fly, or you're doing more of a hobby that you love. Really get a feel for what you want and put down absolutely everything that you can think of.

Now, what does your clinic need to do to provide you with that standard of living (and remember that this stuff doesn't have to be paid for outright – although it can of course).

What profits do you need to generate? What turnover is required? And what staffing levels? What are the positions you need in those staffing levels? What premises do you need and do you own them? Do you need more than one premises? Do you need to be based in different locations? Think about everything that your business will require at that point.

And now write out where you are today in terms of both your lifestyle and your business, and where you'll need to be in roughly three years for all the areas we've already got on the sheet.

Step Two, Build Your Overall Clinic's Strategy
Your strategy is there to give you a feel for what's happening within your clinic over these next five years. Work out each year on a flip chart pad or large piece of paper, and build up the picture of everything that's going on. Start at the five year point and work backwards. You can even use post-it notes if you want, that way you can take them off if it doesn't look right as you build your picture.

Start with your profit and turnover then look at all the different areas of your business such as marketing, sales, premises, staff, distribution, target clients, geographical areas, operational challenges, product areas, product percentages… To make it as easy as possible for you, I've produced a list of things below and shared some specifics that you may want to include in your strategy diagram:

Marketing

Think back to the marketing plan section where we asked you to build up an avatar for your ideal clients. Where are you marketing? Where are your competitors advertising? Is there somewhere else your clients are that they've missed? Are there any awards you need to be going for? What kind of PR are you doing to raise your profile? How is your marketing building over the next few years? How many different marketing strategies are you going to need (and remember, you must track them all). Are you going international?...

Product or Services

What products or services are you going to be offering? How many different types? How are these going to change as time moves on? What bolt-ons, upgrades, or added-value items are you going to add to them?...

Distribution

What percentage of the products or services you're offering account for your clinic's turnover? It may be that you're looking to increase the percentage of a certain service because it's more profitable, for example…

Geographic Areas

Which areas are you looking to focus on? Are you staying in your own county, district or state? If so, which towns are you targeting first? Or are you going wider? Which regions of the country are core to you? And how is that going to develop over the next few years? Are you going international?...

Operations

What kind of staff, services or production systems are you

going to develop? What size and scope? And what are the potential issues?

Premises

Are you in rented premises or have you bought your own? What size of premises do you need for your staffing or production requirements and when will this need to change from present-day? Would a purpose-built facility be an advantage? And do you need to move to a certain area to help with recruitment, for distribution reasons, or to benefit from better road and rail links?

Sales

Is the first step to develop a sales process and scripts? Do you need to set up how you're going to track and measure success? Will you attend sales trainings, and if so which ones and focused on what? How many sales staff are you going to employ?...

Customers

Who are your customers? Where are they located? How many of them are there? Do you have ten small ones then two really large ones, or twenty massive ones straight away? (Remember to make sure that at no time is your business at the mercy of just one major customer – if you bring on a customer that's 30% of your business, well done, but feel panicked enough to go and get another one of an equal or even larger size so that if they left you, you wouldn't be in trouble.)

Funding Issues

Where is the funding for growth coming from? How much do you need? Is the business producing enough or are you going to need outside investment? What do you need to do now to be able to secure that funding in the future?

Start from where you'll be in five years' time and work your way to present day. And try to think how each different area will affect each other area of the business. After doing this, one client I worked with realised that he'd actually need to move premises within 18 months because his production was going to outstrip the area he had available to work in. And with timings as they were, he actually only had six months from our strategy day to find somewhere.

Without thinking ahead and planning like this, it may have been a year before he realised and then he'd certainly have experienced some pain – whether struggling to get premises and move in time, or having to slow down production or turn work away because his existing site couldn't cope.

So, looking at where you are now, look at what you need to be doing next year. Do you need to hire administrative staff? Move premises to become more efficient? Give your staff more training or a pay rise? Will there be additional costs such as utilities? Will you be moving to an even higher standard of work, or will you secure accreditation so that you can charge more? Perhaps you'll aim to get the cost of sales down by a few percent. Or, if you're purchasing more, you may wish to negotiate a better deal or a discount from your suppliers....

If you can't make the figures work on paper its unlikely that you'll make them work in real life, so go back to the drawing board and start again until it does all add up. And also do just be aware of what we term 'crackernomics'™ when you're setting your figures. Many of us will have seen a Dragon's Den episode where an entrepreneur is pitching their idea to the Dragons and values their business in the £multiple-millions despite them doing limited research, not yet launching – or often even making – a product, and without boasting any assets at all. Dream big when it comes to lifestyle, but apply a reality check when it comes to your business statistics.

Now that you've got a rough map of what you're doing for the next three to five years, leave that in sight for the moment so you can refer back to it. I'd suggest sticking it on a wall somewhere prominent.

Step Three, Plan and Analysis

This is where we look at the overall strategy you've just built up and start to lay out what needs to be done in the clinic to achieve these targets.

So, look at each of the areas you've just worked through, such as marketing, staffing, and premises, and using your flip chart paper to start making a list of things that need to be done, and all the opportunities that come along with that (so, for example, you might need to get some sort of accreditation within your industry to charge more for your services). Do this for every area.

Once you have all the things that you need to do, start to think about what challenges there are around those things you need to achieve, and list those out on another flip chart page. You might, for example, need to spend £10,000 training someone to achieve your accreditation, and you may also then be at risk of them leaving the business. Again, do this for every area we've covered in your business.

Once this is done you'll have a pretty good feel for what needs to be achieved, and what some of the potential challenges could be on this journey, so we shouldn't get too many nasty surprises. Particularly as the next step should take care of pretty much everything on this list…

Step Four, Build Your Action List

Now that you've completed the analysis, we can start to build a plan of how we're actually going to drive your business forward on a day-to-day basis. So, you can now move away from the flip chart and use an old-fashioned pen and paper and, looking at your plan and analysis, consider what action you can take about each of the things you've written down. So, if you have a real need to get that accreditation, write it on your action list and consider whether there any other accreditations you should be thinking about too…

Now, move on to the potential challenges that you've noted, and consider these in more detail. In our example of gaining accreditation, the cost might be a challenge but then you have to look at the return on investment over the long term. We also mentioned that the person you train might decide to leave, so what can you do to get them to commit to your business, and what can you offer them?

The idea is to either take action about something or accept it as it is. For example, if you've put down a meteor hitting the earth as a challenge to your business, there's probably not much you can do about that so you may have to accept that for what it is. However, if one of the challenges was that you're in a partnership and you still haven't got a shareholders' agreement and cross-party options done, then that absolutely must be listed for action.

Build up a list of things that you need to do to ultimately get you to the lifestyle you want, and don't hold back. Think of how you can achieve these things, and not the reasons why it wouldn't happen to you. Also, go back over the strategy you built for the business and see if there is anything on there that you need to transfer as an action, just in case you've missed something.

And when you've done all of that… take a break! Your head might be slightly frazzled but the last few hours will have been amongst the most valuable that you've spent on your business to date.

Step Five, Pulling It All Together

Okay, so you now need to transfer the overall clinic Strategy and your Plan from the flip chart onto paper so you can refer back to them. For the clinic's Strategy I'd suggest writing it out as a timeline so you can see how the business builds up and how all the different pieces fit together. I'd also suggest printing two copies of each of these, one for a folder and one for the wall.

Now, we also really need to start building your list of actions for the next year, and I've produced another free resource to help here, a Project Log which you can download from www.TheBeautifulBusinessBook.com. Look at what you've produced, and what needs to be achieved by the end of the year for you to hit your targets.

Again, using our securing accreditation example, you might have a few tasks to complete that require action, like selecting the right person for training, offering incentives to tie them into the business, raising funding… These tasks will need to be completed in a certain order and you can set them out on a month-by-month basis.

I've included a Project Plan and a Break Through Line of Sight Plan, that you can also download for free on **www.TheBeautifulBusinessBook.com** so do make use of either of these – it's down to personal choice. You can then start to build up a picture of how these actions across the whole business start to tie in together. Once you've set out the actions and tasks, you can also print off these pages and put them in your folder or even on the wall.

In your folder you should now have a Business Plan that you can look at. It won't be one of those huge business plans or tick-box exercises that sit on a shelf and gather dust. Rather, it'll be a practical and dynamic one page clinic Strategy. Your Plan shares your targets for the next five years, and your one

or two-page Project Log shows your actions for the next
phase of your growth.

Small Changes for Huge Results

You'll sometimes hear people saying 'if only this would happen' or 'if only we could get that we'd be made'. Well, I hate to tell you, but in my experience there is no silver bullet for any clinic. No 'if only', and no 'one answer or action to building a great clinic'. It's about small changes across every area, so let's look at these and give you a worked example…

As a reminder and to demonstrate the importance of all we've covered, what we're going to look at is how focusing specifically on each area of our business in turn can show potentially huge opportunities to increase turnover:

First we have **the number of clients** that are currently purchasing from you. This is anyone who is within the purchasing cycle of your goods or services, but you also have to think about anyone who has ever bought from you. If you've been going for a while, you're going to have people's details somewhere. Do you have a database? If not, perhaps you could look at old invoices to secure this information and you could then transfer it onto a database as that will allow you to get in touch again.

Trust me, this is one area you really don't want to fall down on, as your financial future depends on having up-to-date details for anyone that you've ever come into contact with. And when I say anyone, I mean everyone. So, if they've phoned you, browsed your website, walked through your door, asked for information, bought from you online, or ever caught your attention, you need to capture their details. Bear in mind legal and best practice guidance of course though, and always give people the opportunity to unsubscribe from any communications.

And do remember that an average 68% of your clients leave because of perceived indifference in that they simply don't think you care. So, whatever you do, make sure they feel the love no matter how long it takes them to come back.

New Leads is any potential new business that comes your way via whatever marketing methods you're focusing on. It could be emails, phone calls, quotes, referrals, or people simply walking through your door. And just going back to the database, do your absolute best to capture these potential customers' details and put them on to your database.

Converting New Leads is the actual percentage of new clients that you get to hand over money and become one of your lucky new customers.

Average Number of Purchases Each Year is how often your clients return to you.

And the **Average Value of Each Purchase** is the total value of your sales divided by the total number of your customers, to give you an average spend.

So, looking at these figures what we're going to do is increase each one by 10%. Not a huge number by any stretch, and using the tactics we have talked about you should be able to do this easily in your business. In fact, when you stop to think, it's simply small steps like getting your conversion ratio from 25% to 27.5%, so we're really not asking too much.

Customers	25	35
New Leads	40	44
Converting Leads	25%	27.5%
Total Customer Now	35	47.1
Average Purchases PA	7.1	7.8
Purchase Average Value	£710	£781
TOTAL SALES	£176,435	£286,923

As you can see here, the small changes noted in the right hand column – across the whole business – result in an increase of £110,488 or about a 40% uplift in sales! Remember earlier how we were talking about 70% of businesses never make it into that lifestyle business that so many want, it literally is just lots of small tweaks that will get you to where you want to be.

I sincerely wish every success to you, your family, and your business. I'd love to stay in touch if you want to, and to hear about your successes using the tools in this book. As I develop new programmes and support that will be of use to you I'll let you know, and if you want to be added to the prestigious ranks of *The Beautiful Business Success Board*, do send me a picture and a few lines about where you were and where you are now. You can also follow me on Pinterest (AlanHorizons) for business tips and insights, inspirational words, and my own favourite resources like must-watch TED talks.

Have a great year and here's wishing you every success with your plan, your focus, and getting the life you deserve.

About The Author

A former weapons engineer and submariner with the Royal Navy, Alan S Adams now channels his expertise to get beneath the surface of business strategy in his role as Founder and Director of Horizons Consultants.

A Master Neuro-Linguistic Programming (NLP) practitioner and fully qualified life coach, Alan has a real passion for understanding business, which was ignited when he studied for a BSc Degree in International Disaster Engineering and Management where he focused on companies' and governments' strategies to deal with crises.

He now uses these skills to provide strategic support, to coach and train business owners across the length and breadth of the UK, in particular small and medium-sized enterprises. Alan runs a series of seminars, workshops, and interactive sessions where business owners can receive practical advice and guidance in areas such as increasing business profitability and cash flow, goal-setting, and business growth. He also works with companies on a more strategic level, where he conducts a complete top to bottom review, and then works with business owners to analyse their strengths and weaknesses, before putting in place and delivering bespoke business development plans.

Shropshire born and bred, and now living in Telford, Alan is something of an adrenaline junkie. He is a keen snowboarder and motorcyclist, and also enjoys taking part in outdoor activities such as skydiving.

www.ingramcontent.com/pod-product-compliance
Lightning Source LLC
Chambersburg PA
CBHW061539050726
47593CB00002B/834